W9-CIG-680

THE GREAT
HISPANIC HERITAGE

America Ferrera

THE GREAT HISPANIC HERITAGE

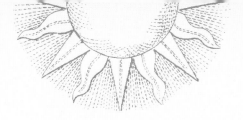

THE GREAT
HISPANIC HERITAGE

America Ferrera

Dennis Abrams

CHELSEA HOUSE
PUBLISHERS
An imprint of Infobase Publishing

America Ferrera

Copyright © 2010 by Infobase Publishing

Chelsea House
An imprint of Infobase Publishing
132 West 31st Street
New York NY 10001

Library of Congress Cataloging-in-Publication Data
Abrams, Dennis, 1960-
  America Ferrera / Dennis Abrams.
    p. cm. — (Great Hispanic heritage)
  Includes bibliographical references and index.
  ISBN 978-1-60413-967-9 (hardcover)
 1. Ferrera, America, 1984—Juvenile literature. 2. Actors—United States—Biography—Juvenile literature. 3. Hispanic American actors—Biography—Juvenile literature. I. Title. II. Series.
  PN2287.F423A27 2010
  791.4302'8092—dc22
  [B]   2010009481

Text design by Terry Mallon
Cover design by Terry Mallon/Keith Trego
Composition by EJB Publishing Services
Cover printed by Bang Printing, Brainerd, MN
Book printed and bound by Bang Printing, Brainerd, MN
Date printed: September 2010
Printed in the United States of America

10 9 8 7 6 5 4 3 2 1

Contents

Yo Soy Betty, La Fea

In Colombia, it's called *Yo soy Betty, la fea* ("I am Betty, the ugly"). In India, it's called *Jassi Jaissi Koi Nahin* ("There's No One Like Jassi"). In Turkey, *Sensiz Olmuyor*. In Germany, it's called *Verliebt in Berlin*. Russians know it as *Ne Rodis' Krasivoy* ("Be Not Born Beautiful," from the popular Russian saying "Be not born beautiful, but be born happy"). In Mexico, it's *La Fea Mas Bella* ("The Most Beautiful Ugly Woman").

In Spain, it's *Yo Soy Bea* ("I Am Bea"), a pun, with the word *Bea* sounding much like *fea*, which means "ugly." In Greece, it's called *Maria, I Aschimi* ("Maria, The Ugly One"). Belgians know it simply as *Sara*. In Serbia-Croatia, it's *Ne daj se, Nina* ("Don't Give Up Nina"). Czech Republic? It's *Osklivka Katka*—"Ugly Kate." Vietnam? *Co gai xau xi*. The Philippines? *I Love Betty La Fea*. China? *Chou Nu Wu Di* ("Ugly Wudi," which literally means "The Ugly Without Rival"). Poland? *BrzydUla*.

And in the United States, it's known simply as *Ugly Betty*.

Clearly, under whatever name you'd like to call it, the television show *Ugly Betty* is a worldwide phenomenon, one that has struck a chord and brought pleasure to many television viewers. Before it became a phenomenon, however, *Ugly Betty* started out its life more simply, as just one more telenovela shown on Colombian television.

According to the Museum of Broadcast Communications, the *telenovela* is a "form of melodramatic serialized fiction produced and aired in most Latin American countries."[1] Telenovelas are some of the most popular programs shown on Latin American television, as every night millions upon millions of viewers tune in to watch the latest trials and tribulations of their favorite heroes and heroines. The programs tend to be highly romantic, focusing on the relationship between couples as the basis for much of the shows' plot development. The Peruvian telenovela *Simplemente Maria*, for example, was an example of a modern-day Cinderella story, set against a backdrop of the problems of migration into the big city. The Brazilian telenovela *Beto Rockefeller* told the story of a simple man who worked at a shoe shop while at the same time pretending to be a millionaire, and getting involved with two very different women: one rich, the other poor.

But in 1999, viewers of Colombia's television channel RCN (Radio Cadena Nacional) got their first glimpse of a new kind of telenovela, *Yo soy Betty, la fea*. It was different from any other show most people had ever seen, and it was, in its way, a truly groundbreaking event, one that showed an entirely different look at women than had traditionally been shown on Latin American television. Sandra Hernandez, writing for Salon.com in 2001, explained the cultural shockwave that was "Betty La Fea: "Telenovelas . . . have . . . maintained a traditional view of women's aspirations, one that equates female success with being beautiful and married. While there have been a few exceptions . . . soaps have mostly remained faithful to a single plot involving a beautiful ingénue's search for love.

America Ferrera promotes her hit television show, *Ugly Betty*. The show brought the talented young actress into the living rooms of millions of Americans.

It was against this backdrop that Betty the Ugly One began. . . . With her thick glasses, braces and unibrow, Betty wasn't much to look at, by Latin standards. Her poor sense of style, squeaky voice and intelligence only made her plight that much more desperate. . . . The premise was stunning: a woman whose appeal is her intelligence, humanity and humor struggles to be seen, heard, and, ultimately adored."[2]

The series, which ran for just two years, from 1999 to 2001, for a total of 338 half-hour and 160-hour episodes, tells a story familiar to anyone who has seen the American version, *Ugly Betty*. In it, Beatriz Aurora Pinzon Solano, otherwise known as Betty, is an unattractive (but brilliant) economist working as a secretary for the fictitious Colombian fashion empire EcoModa. There, Betty faces the constant scorn and wrath of the company's manager-owners, but proves her worth to EcoModa's new president, the devastatingly attractive Armando Mendoza, by becoming his accomplice in a plan to save EcoModa from financial ruin. And, of course, in the midst of it all, the two fall in love.

The show was an instant smash, within months earning the ratings of all other programs being aired in Colombia combined, and had been sold to two other countries in the area. Betty's honesty and integrity made her a heroine to millions, because, as former Colombian Vice President Carlos Lemos Simmonds commented:

> In Latin America, where calamities are commonplace and prosperity is the exception, the anti-hero is the triumph of the genuine over the artificial ... Betty Pinzon is just that. (She) comes from a world ... where principles like loyalty and honor still matter. And she tries to make her way in another world, the world of "beautiful people" ... where greed and cynicism rule.[3]

Obviously, the triumph of "the genuine over the artificial" was something that appealed to audiences in other countries besides Colombia. After its initial success in Colombia, the series aired on Telemundo, an American-based Spanish language television network. It soon spread throughout the world. In some countries, the original Colombian version was shown dubbed into the local language; in other countries, as we have seen, new versions were filmed, with the stories and characters adapted to fit their new locations.

At the height of its international popularity, the show was airing in over 70 countries in more than 2 billion homes worldwide. In the United States, the original Colombian version, *Yo soy Betty*, aired on the Spanish-speaking channel Telemundo, but the English-language networks didn't pay it much attention. But, as Telemundo's ratings began to improve, especially in cities with large Latin American communities such as Los Angeles, Miami, and New York, attention increased.

As the nation's Latin American population continued to climb, it seemed likely that it was only a matter of time before the major television networks would begin to create programming that reflected their changing audience. And at the same time, one of Hollywood's leading Latin American actresses was wondering how she could bring *Yo soy Betty* to American audiences.

SALMA HAYEK

Born and raised in Mexico, Salma Hayek grew up wanting desperately to become an actress. But with her strikingly beautiful dark features and full-figured body, she didn't fit into the stereotype of the delicate and ladylike female actress so beloved by Latin American directors. It seems that, no matter where one grows up, there are always stereotypes that need to be overcome.

She was constantly told "You'll never make it."[4] But she persevered, winning roles in Mexican telenovelas that proved her worth as an actress. At the age of just 23, she won a TV Novela (the equivalent of an American Emmy award) as Best Newcomer, for her starring role in the telenovela *Teresa*.

Hollywood, always on the lookout for a beautiful woman who can act, came calling in the person of director Robert Rodriguez. Rodriguez, a native of Mexico, cast Hayek opposite Antonio Banderas in his film *Desperado*, in which Hayek caused a small sensation. Other parts soon followed, including the hit movies *Spy Kids* and *From Dusk Till Dawn*.

Still, she wanted more, and in the year 2000, Hayek founded the film production company *Ventanarosa* ("Rose-colored window"), through which she could produce both

Salma Hayek makes a call from the set of *Ugly Betty*. After buying U.S. rights to the television show that had become a worldwide hit, Hayek worked for years to find a network that would allow her to produce it. America Ferrara had so impressed Hayek when they met years earlier that Hayek pursued the young actress for the title role.

film and television projects, giving her not only more control of her career but also the ability to produce and promote projects with other Latin American actors, directors, and writers.

The first film produced by her company, *El Coronel No Tiene Quien Le Escriba* ("No One Writes to the Colonel"), was Mexico's official selection for submission as Best Foreign Film at the Academy Awards. *Frida*, a film biography of legendary Mexican artist Frida Kahlo and her husband, Diego Rivera, was not only produced by Hayek's company but starred the actress as well, making her the first Mexican actress to ever receive an Academy Award nomination for best actress.

Hayek obviously had a talent not only for acting but also for finding and producing projects that could receive both critical and popular success. Always on the lookout for new projects, Hayek had never forgotten her roots in Latin American telenovelas and watched them regularly, hoping for inspiration to strike. And, as soon as she saw *Yo soy Betty* she knew she had found her next project. "The original was groundbreaking," she told *BBC News*. "I immediately jumped on it."[5]

Hayek bought the U.S. rights to the show in 2001, but getting the show off the ground was easier said than done. She spent the next several years going from executive producer to executive producer, asking them to take on the show. But for two years, despite her own success as an actress, she couldn't find anyone interested in putting on the air the story of a homely girl working in the high-powered world of high fashion.

Then, NBC seemed to be interested. But shortly thereafter, the network backed out. Hayek was not willing to give up. Believing in the project, she took greater control, and instead of attempting to find someone else to produce the show, she decided to do it herself. It turned out to be the best decision she could possibly make.

Hayek had been working in Hollywood for nearly 10 years by that point, and she decided to go all out, using all her contacts and pulling out all the stops to get her pet project on the air. By attaching herself to the project in such a personal way, the idea for the show began to get noticed, as television executives finally began to catch on to the show's potential. As Hayek's producing partner Ben Silverman told the *Toronto*

FRIDA KAHLO

If actress Salma Hayek, who received rave reviews and an Academy Award nomination for playing artist Frida Kahlo, is known for her beauty, Kahlo herself is known for combining artistic talent with her own distinct looks to become one of the best-known female artists of the twentieth century.

Born on July 6, 1907, Kahlo contracted polio at the age of six, which left her right leg thinner than the left. At the age of 18, she was riding a bus that collided with a trolley car —Kahlo suffered serious injuries in the accident, including a broken spinal column, a broken collarbone, broken ribs, a broken pelvis, 11 fractures in her right leg, a crushed and dislocated right foot, and a dislocated shoulder. An iron handrail also pierced her abdomen and her uterus, seriously damaging her ability to have children.

But despite a lifetime of nearly unbelievable pain, Kahlo persevered, creating some of the most memorable art of her time, using bright colors and mixing both Mexican and European influences to create a style uniquely her own. Perhaps her best-known works are a series of self-portraits that bravely confront the world with her pain. Little known in her own lifetime, today Kahlo is a feminist icon, treasured both for her art and her struggles to make her art. On June 21, 2001, Kahlo became the first Hispanic woman to receive the honor of having her face on a U.S. postage stamp.

Star, the story of Ugly Betty was universal. "It is *Cinderella*. It is *My Fair Lady*. It has worked a thousand times in a thousand places in a thousand ways and it was a story we really wanted to tell."[6]

Finally, on May 26, 2006, ABC announced that *Ugly Betty* would be a part of its 2006–2007 North American season lineup as a weekly series. (Initially, ABC announced that the title would be *Betty the Ugly*, but changed it to *Ugly Betty* on July 14.) Now that Hayek had convinced ABC to air the program, all she had to do was find the right actress to play the role.

Fortunately for her, the choice was an easy one. Years earlier, Hayek had been on the set of *The Oprah Winfrey Show*, where she had been introduced to an up-and-coming young actress named America Ferrera, who was there talking about her film *Real Women Have Curves*. It was love at first sight: "I saw [America] and I got to talk to her, and I just completely fell in love with her. I knew she was a superstar and I made a mental note in my head, one day I'm going to work with her. So when the opportunity came, the first person on my mind was her."[7]

To most Americans, America Ferrera was still a little-known actress who had starred in a couple of low-budget films and guest-starred on some very popular television shows. But within weeks of *Ugly Betty*'s premiere on September 28, 2006, America Ferrera was one of the country's hottest actresses, seen on magazine covers and talk shows from coast to coast. Within a year, she had won every major acting award possible for her role as Betty.

How did she get there? How did America Ferrera, the daughter of Honduran immigrants, go from an unknown to a superstar in what seemed like the blink of an eye? It's a fascinating story, as Ferrera climbed the ranks of Hollywood stardom and changed the rules for what it means to be a Latin American actress in the United States.

Latinos in Hollywood

For as long as there have been actors in Hollywood, there have been Latino and Latina actors in Hollywood. But what is interesting is how, as the years have passed, their prominence and the kinds of roles they have been offered have changed.

In the early days of Hollywood, for example, in the era of silent films, a large number of stars were Latinos. They performed using very Spanish-sounding surnames: Ramon Navarro, Dolores del Rio, Raquel Torres, and Lupe Velez were some of the big stars of the period.

But by the 1950s and 1960s, the only "Spanish"-sounding names belonged to actors who played the traditional Latin lover—a character who often did not end up with the non-Latina leading lady in his arms. And, as Clara Rodriguez points out in her book *Heroes, Lovers, and Others: The Story of Latinos in Hollywood*, "There were Latino characters in films like *West Side Story* (1961) and other gang movies, but they were generally played by non-Latino actors. Often, the Latino characters in westerns were the bad guys, the nameless "banditos," or the cantina girls who had little time or substantial presence on the screen. . . . Television brought in Desi Arnaz (as Ricky Ricardo) and guest appearances by Carmen Miranda, as well as *The Cisco Kid* and *Zorro* series, but they were the exceptions. Although these positive characters spoke to Latinos and the rest of America, they did not speak *about* Latinos in the United States. . . . In addition, most Hollywood stars hid their ethnic origins. Ethnicity was seldom talked about on television or in most movie magazines . . . No, leading Hollywood stars had names like Elizabeth Taylor, John Wayne, and Grace Kelly."[1] Obviously, Hollywood has come a long way from those stereotypical roles to today's Latina stars such as America Ferrera. But, how and why have the roles of Latinos in Hollywood changed so much over the years?

THE SILENT DAYS

In the early days of Hollywood, the early years of the twentieth century, the term *Latino* didn't exist. The term then was *Latin*, which was used not only to describe actors from the Spanish-speaking Americas (Mexico, Central America, and South America) but also, actors from Portugal and Spain as well. Rudolph Valentino, the original "Latin" lover who effectively started the craze for "Latin" movie stars, was actually from Italy!

Valentino was so popular that when he died at the peak of his career, every available "Latin" or Latino actor was promoted as his successor. Valentino's fame was so huge that even Latina actresses got swept into the craze, as studios all began looking for their own "female Valentino." The search brought such actors as Dolores del Rio and Lupe Velez, both popular stars in their native Mexico, to the United States and stardom.

There were other factors at work as well. There was, at the same time, a newly born fascination in the United States with all things Mexican. Pre-colonial Mexican history, contemporary artists such as muralist Diego Rivera, and even Mexican music all became topics of interest and conversation. And, as Clara Rodriguez points out, that craze for all things Mexican extended to Hollywood films as well: "In the Hollywood

Carmen Miranda was a popular Latina singer and actress known for her outrageous fruit headdress. She was the highest-paid entertainer in Hollywood in the mid-1940s. Despite Miranda's success, being accepted in Hollywood remained difficult for Latinas.

media, lace mantillas, Spanish combs, ruffled lace dresses, dark sultry looks, pulled-back hair with 'Spanish' side curls, toreador [bullfighter] themes and clothes, and flamenco poses were prevalent, as were references to 'Spanish' architecture, furniture, personages, places, and customs (bullfights, in particular) . . . However awkwardly defined or understood, the popularity of 'all things Latin' encouraged the adoption and promotion of the 'Latin look.'"[2]

Of course, the fact that the films were silent helped contribute to the employability of so-called Latin actors and actresses—their accents were not an issue if you couldn't actually hear them speak. There is also speculation that the popularity of Latino actors and actresses was helped by the fact that films were in black and white: Because of the high-contrast of those films, shades of color were less important, and so the darker skin of Latino actors actually appeared whiter on film.

But even with their popularity, Latina actresses still tended to fit into stereotypical roles. One exception to that rule was Dolores del Rio, a great beauty known as the first Latina superstar. She was generally cast in a variety of roles that emphasized not so much her ethnic background, but her aristocratic looks and poise. Even so, she found herself frustrated by how the stories of the Latino people were told in Hollywood, saying, "I'd love to appear in fine emotional dramas . . . and am eager to play in stories concerning my native people, the Mexican race. It is my dearest wish to make fans realize their real beauty, their wonder, their greatness as a people. The vast majority seem to regard Mexicans as a race of bandits, or laborers, dirty, unkempt and uneducated. My ambition is to show the best that's in my nation."[3]

Eventually, Del Rio became so frustrated with the roles being offered to her in Hollywood that she left altogether and returned to Mexico in 1943. There, she became known as the First Lady of Mexican theater, as well as The Princess of Mexico, and received numerous awards for her work, including Mexico's equivalent to the Oscar, three times.

More typical of the Latina who became a Hollywood star was Mexican actress Lupe Velez, who became known as the Mexican spitfire. While Del Rio's persona was exotic, Velez's was much more "ethnic," playing what was seen then as a "typical" Latina woman—sexual and quick to anger—a fast-talking "hot tamale."

DISAPPEARING FROM VIEW

But by the late 1930s and into the 1940s, America's love affair with "exotic" Latinos and Latinas seemed to be over. With the outbreak of World War II came the growth in popularity of the "all-American" girl, who was decidedly nonethnic and nonexotic. With few exceptions, leading roles for actors of Hispanic descent began to disappear.

In their place arose a new stereotypical role—that of the cheerful, musical Latin. Typical of that new view of Latinos was actress Carmen Miranda. Although a respected actress and singer in her native Brazil, she found herself unhappily typecast (although well paid) during her time in Hollywood: "Her platform shoes, sparkling smile, radiant personality, energetic and rhythmic dancing and singing—and, perhaps most memorable, her exotic headdresses—made for a signature style that has often been imitated and parodied."[4] Despite her talent, the character that Carmen Miranda played in movie after movie became almost a cartoon—every stereotype of the musical Latina type rolled up into one large-hatted persona.

AFTER THE WAR

With the end of World War II and the beginnings of the Cold War, Hollywood turned even further away from any interest in examining the lives of minority groups, including Latinos. So what was left for Latino and Latina actors? The usual stereotypes: For the men, Latin lovers; for the women, bombshells, spitfires, and sultry Latinas, the ones that "audiences yearned to touch, lusted after, the ones their mothers had warned them about; they made their viewers' hearts skip a beat."[5] The problem was that Latinos and Latinas are much more than just lovers and bombshells. By making those the only roles available and the only ones seen by non-Latino viewers, in movies or on television, the stereotyped role became, in the eyes of many, the only reality they'd ever known—and the image became the reality.

A case in point was Latina actress Rita Moreno. She was "habitually cast as a Latin bombshell, spitfire, or sultry Latina and had to struggle against the limitations of this typecasting. In *Untamed* (1955), for example, she was cast as a 'fiery love machine'; another writer called her a 'Puerto Rican firecracker.'"[6]

"THE LADY IN THE TUTTI FRUTTI HAT"

Carmen Miranda made only 15 movies during her Hollywood career, but of those, perhaps the best known, best remembered, and best loved is the 1943 classic *The Gang's All Here*.

In it, Miranda plays a nightclub performer named "Dorita." Playing the part wasn't an acting challenge for her, but she did get the opportunity to perform in what is probably her greatest musical number: "The Lady in the Tutti-Frutti Hat." Miranda sang lyrics that include "Americanos tell me that my hat is high/ Because I will not take it off to kiss a guy/But if I ever start to take it off, ay, ay!/I do that once for Johnnie Smith/And he is very happy with/The lady in the tutti frutti hat!" while wearing an enormously tall hat completely covered with fruit. The scene created the iconic image she is known for today, an image that became a stereotypical one for Latina women everywhere.

But why a hat covered with fruit? In the Bahia region of Brazil where Miranda grew up, women were often seen in the markets balancing large baskets of fruit on their head, making it easier for them to transport. So she took the idea, and from towering fruit baskets to towering fruit hats, a star was born!

But an aspiring actress has to work no matter what, so for the 14 films she made in the first 11 years of her career, she accepted the stereotypical roles she was offered. As she said, she played all the roles the same way, "barefoot with my nostrils flaring."[7] Even after receiving an Academy Award for best supporting actress in the classic film musical *West Side Story* (1961), the only roles she was offered were "the conventional Rosita and Pepita type roles."[8]

Moreno left Hollywood to work in other performing venues, going on to become the first Latina not only to win an Academy Award, but one of the few actors of *any* ethnicity to win the four top entertainment awards: Oscar (for films), Tony (for Broadway stage), Emmy (for television), and Grammy (for recording).

But in order to accomplish that, Moreno had to leave Hollywood, which still seemed capable of nothing more than casting Latinos and Latinas (when they were cast at all) in stereotypical and often demeaning roles. For young Hispanics growing up in the United States, it was an odd experience to watch television during that period and not see anybody like yourself on the screen. Actor John Leguizamo remembered, "When I was a kid, I never saw any Hispanics on television. And because you never see anything, you start to wonder, God, maybe as a people we can't do it."[9]

Things did slowly start to change in the 1970s and 1980s, but not always for the better. "As Latinos increased in number in the United States and the barrio became the predominant backdrop in most films featuring Latino characters, the representation of 'legitimately' affluent Latinos (that is, other than drug lords) declined. Few upper-class Latino characters appeared in contemporary movies, and fewer still had attained their wealth through legal means. Urban 'bandito' characters—drug lords, dope dealers, and junkies—set against inner-city backdrops prevailed, and the seed of the violent, lower-class criminal blossomed in the

Rita Moreno (*center*) is the only person of Hispanic origin to win the four most prestigious awards in entertainment: the Oscar, Grammy, Emmy, and Tony. In 1961, the Puerto Rican-born Moreno dazzled audiences as Anita in the film *West Side Story*, a still from which is shown here. Her exceptional career, which has spanned five decades, has inspired many young Hispanic performers.

seventies, when the crime and the violence associated with them escalated."[10]

And if Latino men were seen more and more as drug addicts, dealers, and people outside the law, Latina characters both in film and on television continued to be seen, if they were young and beautiful, as sexual characters only, and if older, as careworn mothers, worrying about their drug-addicted sons and sexually driven daughters. The vast panorama of contemporary Hispanic life, the lives and cares of everyday Latino families, was nowhere to be seen.

There were of course exceptions to the rules. With the growth of independent films, of filmmakers beginning to make films outside the traditional studio system, non-stereotypical Hispanic roles began to be seen. And, as the nation's Latino population continued to grow, Hollywood finally began to find ways to reach out to an audience eager to see themselves both in movies and on television.

New Latina stars such as Sonia Braga and Maria Conchita Alonso made their mark on television as well as in movies. Another popular star, Rosie Perez, first became famous as a dancer on the television show *In Living Color* before acting in such movies as *Do the Right Thing*, *White Men Can't Jump*, and *Fearless*, for which she received an Academy Award nomination.

But even with the rapidly changing roles for Latinas in Hollywood, Perez still found herself constantly fighting for better roles. "The quantity of offers has increased," she told a reporter after receiving her Oscar nomination, "but the quality is pretty awful."[11] Perez added that people saw all her roles as being the same, simply because the character was Hispanic. When asked if she feared being stereotyped as a "feisty, foul-mouthed, working-class Latina," Rosie replied, "All the time."[12]

Again, like Rita Moreno more than 30 years earlier, Perez was able to escape stereotypical roles by taking control of her own career and refusing to play characters that she felt were demeaning to her as a Latina. She coproduced and starred in the film *The 24-Hour Woman*, in which she played a television producer trying, as do women of all ethnicities, to balance work, marriage, and motherhood.

But things *were* getting better, although slowly. Latina actresses began appearing with greater regularity on both television and in the movies, with performers as varied as Penelope Cruz, Jennifer Lopez, Rosario Dawson, Michelle Rodriguez, and Eve Mendes achieving success. And despite the varied roles they were getting, they were still, by and large, also sex symbols, known as much for their beauty as for their acting skills. For a young girl growing up in California named America Ferrera, it wasn't enough: "There are not many Latin-American role models in the entertainment business. You can count them on one hand. I would never see myself reflected."[13]

A definite change, however, was in the air. Latinos were moving from the sidelines and from being seen as a minority in part because of what Clara Rodriguez calls the "Latinization" of America.

> It could be heard in the hit music that was being played—from Ricky Martin's ubiquitous "Livin la Vida Loca" to songs that incorporated Spanish words to songs that fused together Latino rhythms from the Caribbean and Central and South America with more recognizably American styles, like rock, country, rap, pop, and jazz ... Without fully realizing it, Americans were hearing Latin music backgrounds in commercials, TV programs, and films. Spanish words were entering the mass vocabulary without translation—like Arnold Schwarzenegger's "Hasta la vista, baby" in *Terminator* or the Mexican Chihuahua's "Yo quiero Taco Bell" in print ads and on television.[14]

And there was more. McDonald's introduced a dulce de leche McFlurry, a Latin McOmelet, a Chipolte BBQ Snack Wrap, and even a mango dipping sauce for McNuggets. Salsa became the most popular condiment in the United States, surpassing even all-American ketchup in popularity. Cinco de Mayo became a holiday celebrated not only in big cities but also in rural America, as the nation's Latino population continued to expand. In other words, "from soccer to salsa—both the edible and danceable varieties—Latinization was sweeping the country."[15]

As Latin American culture entered mainstream American culture, it became evident that the time was right for a new kind of Latina actress to make her mark. One whose attractiveness was secondary to her talent, to her ability to play a variety of roles from a real woman with curves to a skater groupie named Thunder Monkey to Charlie Brown's sister to a high school student with OCD to a pregnant teen to a certain style-challenged character named Ugly Betty. The time was right for America Ferrera.

Dreaming
the Dream

She was born as America Georgina Ferrera on April 18, 1984, the youngest of six children. Her parents had immigrated to the United States from Honduras in the mid-1970s, and even though America herself was born in the United States, the personal connection she feels to Honduras, a small nation located in Central America, is strong. As she told *The Los Angeles Times*, "When you are a first-generation anything, you have your past which is these roots, and it's a part of you because you're so deeply connected to your relatives."[1]

She grew up in the Woodland Hills section of Los Angeles, a comfortable community located in the southwestern area of the San Fernando Valley. Woodland Hills is the home of many other celebrities, including such well-known names as Lisa Kudrow, Ice Cube, Will Smith, and Freddy Rodriguez, one of Ferrera's *Ugly Betty* costars.

Growing up, Ferrera had no idea that one day she would become a celebrity. Indeed, growing up in Woodland Hills, America could not possibly anticipate the life she would be living. Instead, she lived the life of many other young girls, surrounded by brothers and sisters and loving parents.

But despite this, in other ways, her life *was* different. Woodland Hills was, at the time, predominantly "Anglo." (Today, the population is more than 12 percent Latino.) At times, Ferrera felt like an outsider, growing up around people with lighter skin—people who ate different foods at home and whose parents did not struggle with the language. "As early as second grade I remember feeling really different and isolated. I had the hugest crush on a boy, and my best friend had a crush on him too. One day he said to me, 'I like your best friend more because she's paler and she has freckles.' And it was right then that I began to feel like, Oh wow, I'm different."[2]

Because she grew up in the Valley largely surrounded by non-Latinos, however, America didn't feel connected to the Latino community either. As a matter of fact, because Woodland Hills had (and still has) a large Jewish population, most of her best friends were Jewish. America recalls that "I've never been to a single *quinceañera*" (a coming-of-age celebration held on a Latina's 15th birthday, comparable to a "sweet 16" party). Instead, she says, "When I grew up, I went to tons of bar and bas mitzvahs."[3]

Ferrera became so close to her Jewish friends that at one stage of her life she actually considered converting to Judaism because "it was the cool thing to do."[4] She was, in some ways, living in two worlds. Hanging out with her Jewish friends at school and afterward, she fit in so well that "the Latino kids thought I was this white girl."[5]

Even so, as she said in an interview, "I never had a ton of friends, I always had two or three, but when you have four sisters and a brother all a year apart, you don't really need anyone else to play with."[6] But she lived the life of a Latina at home, speaking Spanish, eating the foods of Central America (empanadas and flan were two of her favorites), and reveling in her close-knit family life. But as America approached her seventh birthday, family life was about to change.

RAISING SEVEN CHILDREN ALONE

Although the Ferrera family had been living in the United States for nearly 15 years, America's father had a difficult time adjusting to his new life. When America was just seven years old, he left to return to Honduras. It was an emotional blow to the seven-year-old, one that took her years to come to terms with, as she later said. "It wasn't easy, but as a kid you find ways to make sense of it. I remember just bits and pieces of that time in my life, but I do remember being so incredibly matter-of-fact. It wasn't until I was older that I thought, 'I never really grieved over that.' And there have been male figures in my life who provided that kind of fatherhood role for longer than he was ever in my life."[7] To date, America Ferrera has not seen or heard from her father since he left her family.

HONDURAN IMMIGRANTS IN THE UNITED STATES

It is estimated that in 2008 there were 890,317 Honduran Americans, nearly 40,000 of whom were living in New York City alone.

And while America Ferrera might be the best known, other Honduran Americans have made their mark in the worlds of art, sports, and journalism. David Archuleta (the runner-up on Season 7 of *American Idol*), actor Jose Zuniga, comedian and writer Carlos Mencia, Univision News journalists Satcha Pretto and Neyda Sandoval, as well as NFL Hall of Fame running back Steve Van Buren can all boast of their Honduran ancestry.

Driven by her mother's strong work ethic and emphasis on education, America Ferrera maintained excellent grades while auditioning and working part-time jobs to pay for acting classes. While she knew she needed to act, her mother maintained hopes that America would become a doctor or a lawyer.

America's mother (also named America) filed for divorce and did what she had to do to raise her family on her own, working long hours as a housecleaning staff director for a Hilton hotel. It was a struggle to support six children (five girls and one boy) on her salary, and the family often subsisted on a simple diet of rice, beans, and tortillas. But although times could sometimes be difficult, today, America has nothing but awe and respect for her mother's achievement: "No matter how much a single mother makes, six mouths is a lot to feed. I don't know how she did it. She's amazing."[8] And despite all the long hours her mother worked at the Hilton, she was always there to provide her children with the love and support they needed. "There was so much love and so much attention placed on what we did have," America told Northjersey.com.[9]

Along with the love and attention came discipline. As an immigrant working a tough job, America's mother appreciated the value of education, and demanded of her children that they apply themselves in school and get the best grades possible. Remarkably, this single mother from Honduras instilled her values into her children so well that all of them graduated from college.

But her youngest daughter, despite realizing the importance of education, had other dreams. Dreams of acting, dreams of stardom, dreams that would eventually set her on a collision course with her mother's dreams for her.

DREAMS OF ACTING

From the beginning, she was a performer. "I always grabbed the video camera or a tape recorder and sat with my friends for hours, making up radio shows."[10] At the age of just seven, America Ferrera knew what she wanted to be when she grew up—a professional actor. She began as most wannabe actors do, trying out for parts in school plays and at her local community theater.

When America was in the third grade, her older sisters came home from school with news: Their junior high school was going to be staging William Shakespeare's *Romeo and Juliet*. Although she was not yet in junior high, America was determined to get a part in the play. Of course, her sisters weren't at all happy about this, telling her "You can't be in our play!"[11] But America, just eight years old, was not to be deterred. She went to the school auditorium, where tryouts were being held, and announced that she was ready to audition!

As she said in an interview with the *Oakland Tribune* years later, it was not an auspicious beginning: "I gave the most horrible audition. [But] the director probably thought I was the cutest thing in the world and gave me a bunch of really small parts . . . It was not anything profound but it was fun, and I just did anything and anywhere."[12] It's that drive, the willingness to do anything that is essential for an actor to succeed.

But what also set Ferrera apart was the early realization that acting wasn't just something she *wanted* to do. It was something she *needed* to do. And it was those first parts in *Romeo and Juliet* (including the part of the apothecary) that convinced her that this was true. "And from then on, it was just like—I just did it because I loved to do it. I don't even think I was aware of an audience."[13]

And, as she said in a 2002 interview with FilmMonthly.com, acting, even in small parts in junior high school productions, made her realize, "That it's something that's inside. I'm a very expressive person and can express myself well. So I choose to use acting as a medium to make change and effect people." Even at the tender age of eight, acting "[w]as an outlet and somewhere I felt like I fit in. Kids are always searching for something where they think they belong and for me it was the drama club or on the stage. It was there that I felt that people could understand me. Latin people in particular are not encouraged to be very emotionally expressive people, just animated. We're very animated, but not a lot of communication goes on between parents and kids."[14] And while there might not be a lot of communication going on between parents and kids, the communication that was going on between America and her mother was anything but positive.

Her mother had other dreams for her daughter, dreams that did not include her becoming an actress. Her dreams for her daughter were bigger and more practical. As with many immigrants, both of America's parents had wanted her to go to college and have a steady, reliable career. "Acting was not

PLAYING HISPANIC

America Ferrera, named one of the 15 most influential Hispanics in the United States by *People en Español* and named Hispanic Woman of the Year by both *Billboard* and the *Hollywood Reporter*, is proud both of her heritage and that through her acting she is able to present a wide range of Hispanic roles to non-Hispanic audiences.

Whether playing Ana Garcia in *Real Women Have Curves*, Carmen in *The Sisterhood of the Traveling Pants*, or Luiza in *Hacia la oscuridad* (*Towards Darkness*), Ferrera is proud that, as a Latina actress, she's able to portray roles that steer clear of the usual stereotypical Hispanic roles so often portrayed in films and television.

Even *Ugly Betty*, while on the surface a show about the world of New York City high fashion, is notable for its honest portrayal of Latino life in America. "It feels good to be part of a show that means more to people than just entertainment, and which confronts a lot of issues, like the portrayal of a Latin family with a father struggling for citizenship," Ferrera said.*

By drawing on her family's Hispanic heritage, and by accepting roles other than those of the traditional "Latina spitfire," America Ferrera has been able to redefine what it means to be a Hispanic American to audiences worldwide.

---

*Sheila Anderson, *America Ferrera: Latina Superstar*. Berkeley Heights. N.J.: Enslow Publishers, Inc., 2009, p. 25.

something that they came to this country to have me do," she explained.[15]

It's not that America's mother didn't love her daughter or want to support her in her dreams. Besides hoping that her daughter would find a "professional" career of some sort, she was also aware of the pitfalls and risks inherent in trying to become an actress. A large part of her opposition was, in fact, born of a desire not to see her youngest daughter hurt by rejection after rejection. As she said years later in an interview with *USA Today*, "My idea was, 'No, I don't like it.' After one bad audition, I said, 'You need to change your mind. You're short. You're Latino. You're not blond. You don't have blue eyes. You won't get into this business.'"[16]

And her mother was right. She was short. She was Latino. She wasn't blond. She didn't have blue eyes. In other words, she did not fit the usual mold for a young actress. But young America Ferrera didn't care. Acting wasn't just something she wanted to do; it was something she *needed* to do. As she told her mother, "'You don't understand. I want to do this like a doctor wants to be a doctor, like a teacher wants to be a teacher.'"[17]

And ironically, it was in part because of her mother that America was determined to become an actress. As America said in an interview, "The way my mother raised me and the values she instilled in me allowed me to be persistent. She taught me you can be whatever you want, no matter what people say."[18]

But, for a time, America's dream seemed to be outside of her reach. She went on audition after audition but with no luck. And, with her mother's insistence that if she was going to be an actress she'd have to do it on her own, America, besides going to school and going out on auditions, worked as a waitress to pay for acting classes and the photographs needed in order to get acting jobs. And to top it off, since her mother was often working, Ferrera was forced to take the bus to get to her auditions.

It was a difficult time for her. She was not getting the roles she was trying out for, and it often seemed that her mother's worst fears were coming true. It quickly became obvious to America that the roles weren't being given to her because of a lack of acting ability, but because of her appearance. It must have been a difficult thing for the aspiring young actress to realize. "I never felt like being Latina was a huge part of my identity until I started going out on auditions. Then people saw me as a Latina. The label was instant."[19]

Not only was she Latina, her body type, that of a healthy young woman, didn't match that of the thin actress then seen as the "ideal." For a teenage girl, struggling with coming to terms with her own self-image, it was a definite blow to the ego. "I didn't even know I was fat until I started acting. I didn't know how fat and ugly I was until I started going on auditions."[20] Imagine the young America Ferrera, desperately wanting to become an actress, auditioning for every part she possibly could, and not getting the job simply because of her looks! Imagine the determination necessary to keep trying despite receiving little to no encouragement. "It was like saying I wanted to go to the moon," she told *USA Today*. "People would say, 'What are you talking about? You don't look like anything special.'"[21]

Now a student at El Camino Real High School, she had signed on with a small talent agency, but the breaks still weren't going her way. But not for lack of trying. As she told the *Chicago Sun-Times*, "I'm the girl who auditioned for everything for a year and never even got a callback."[22] It was hard on a personal level—like most teenage girls, America was well aware of the way she looked and exactly what body type she had. "I went through a lot of self-doubt," she told Elizabeth Weitzman in *Interview*. "I never turned on the TV and saw a Latina woman with an average body and I thought, I'll never be a Charlie's Angel, because I can't fit into size zero leather pants."[23]

Sometimes, as hard as it may be to believe, there were events that were even more painful for Ferrera than getting rejected on the basis of her looks. Sometimes, she didn't even get the opportunity to try out for a part. "It was really heartbreaking the first time I didn't even get to audition for a role that I loved," she told the *Oakland Tribune*.[24] It's not that casting agents didn't respect her talent—they all agreed that she had the skills necessary to become an actress. What was holding her back was not only that she was a Latina actress trying out for parts in what was still an Anglo-dominated Hollywood,

Ferrera's first big break came when she landed a role in the Disney movie, *Gotta Kick It Up!* The experience taught her that achieving her goals would not solve all her problems. In this photo, Ferrera attends the film's screening in July 2002.

but also that she was a Latina with curves. One discussion with a director hit her particularly hard: "It was very straightforward. It was like, 'Look, I would like to give you a shot. I would like to see you knock it out of the park. But the truth is that we need a white girl in this role, and you're not a white girl.' It was like a blow. It hurt because it was the circumstance that I had no control over. I couldn't even blame myself for that. To get rejected before you even get the chance to show whether or not you're good enough is the ultimate form of racism."[25]

Of course, all actors and actresses go through the rejection process, the time when casting directors make their decisions based on myriad reasons, many of which have nothing to do with ability. Still, America was operating under a greater burden than many others trying to get their break, having to also come up against the stereotypes and prejudices facing Latino actors. "As soon as I started acting, it was 'She's too this' or 'Not enough that.' They wanted me to be the pregnant sixteen-year-old or the gangbanger's daughter."[26]

Despite her overwhelming need to be an actress, Ferrera had no interest in playing stereotypes. At times, after one failed audition after another, she considered giving up on her dream and settling into a career that would make her mother happy. "For a time I thought I could be a lawyer. As a kid I even went to law camp at UCLA. They had us watch *My Cousin Vinny*, which was great. But then we went to the courthouse, and we had to do these mock trials, and once I saw what it really meant to be a lawyer, I realized that it wasn't for me. I thought it was like in the movies, like, 'You can't handle the truth!' That kind of thing."[27]

Despite it all, though, she refused to give up. She kept going to school (and got excellent grades), she kept working as a waitress, she kept taking acting classes, and she kept getting on the bus and going to audition after audition. One day, she knew, the right part would come along, somebody would recognize her talent, and she would get the break she deserved.

Finally, at the age of 16, after 10 years of acting in school plays, of endless auditions and endless rejections, America Ferrera got the break she had been hoping for. Casting agents at Disney Productions offered her a part in an upcoming movie to be called *Gotta Kick It Up!* America happily accepted the role, imagining the great parts, the great roles, the great things that would come of it.

Unfortunately, her big break ended up being a big disappointment.

Paying
Her Dues

The film *Gotta Kick It Up!* is a typically upbeat Disney Productions movie that tells the story of a group of Hispanic junior high students who form a dance team and end up at a national competition. America Ferrera would have a lead role, playing Yolanda, a teenage girl whose self-esteem issues get in the way of her performance as a dancer.

It seemed a part tailor-made for her. "I love to dance, so I couldn't believe I was getting paid to just dance all day. And there were four other girls in the cast, so that was fun. And you know the way you think when you're a teenager: Disney Channel today, Oscars tomorrow!"[1] But just a few weeks into filming, Ferrera had what she has since called a "mini nervous breakdown."[2] She has said, "I just felt really empty. I had achieved my dream, and it wasn't totally fulfilling. I still had school problems, and I still had boy problems. My life was still my life. I guess I had been waiting to be turned into a swan."[3]

It's hard to believe, but it's often true: Even when someone has finally achieved what they want, it may not be enough to make them happy. Everyday life, with all its problems, and all its drama, still goes on.

And for America Ferrera, despite grabbing a starring role in a film for Disney, it was still a difficult time, as she said in an interview with *CosmoGIRL!* "My high school days were definitely not the best days of my life. I didn't know who I was. The pretty and the popular girls just reminded me that I wasn't pretty and popular, and the nerdy and studious ones reminded me that I wasn't smart enough. I didn't conform in high school, wear all the right clothes, or fit in."[4]

Still, although painfully aware of her own feelings of loneliness and insecurity, she knew that she wasn't alone in her feelings. "I think the truth is that whatever you're wearing on the outside doesn't change the fact that most people—even beautiful girls—feel the same doubts, fears, and insecurities on the inside."[5]

Those feelings of insecurity would soon be assuaged, or quieted. In the summer before her senior year of high school, America was attending drama camp at Northwestern University in Chicago when she got a call. She was being asked to audition for a part—not just a part, but a starring role in a feature film. It was a part she wanted, a part she could relate to: It was a part that could provide her with the opportunity to prove herself as an actress. Now all she had to do was get the role.

REAL WOMEN HAVE CURVES

Remarkably, the role that America wanted so badly was from a play that had been written more than a decade earlier. That play, *Real Women Have Curves*, had been written by the young playwright Josefina Lopez in 1987, when she was only 19 years old.

The play, set in a tiny sewing factory in East Los Angeles in September of 1987, tells the story of Ana, the youngest employee at the factory. Ambitious and bright, Ana feels trapped working in the factory and wants desperately to escape and go to college, but she doesn't have the money. She also has to contend with her mother, who has been overweight all of her life and is obsessed with Ana's weight. Her mother wants nothing more for her daughter than a "safe" job in the factory, marriage, and family. The action of the play follows Ana, her family, and her friends through the course of one summer at the factory, as the women discuss their lives, loves, desires.

The play is largely autobiographical: Josefina Lopez was a young Mexican-American girl who was born in Mexico but grew up in Los Angeles. She worked in a garment factory with her parents, who did not want her to attend college. And as an actress with "curvy" proportions, she also wrote the play so that she could play the lead role herself, and, in part, to deal with her own issues with her weight. Lopez told an interviewer with the *San Antonio Express-News*, "I wanted to write a play where I was allowed to express my anger at being told constantly that if I lost weight, I would be beautiful."[6]

Producer George LaVoo saw the stage production in 1998 and immediately vowed to get the project filmed. He worked closely with Lopez on a screenplay, but when they brought the completed script to various studios, they were rejected at every turn. Studio executives were certain that nobody would want to see a film about curvy, working-class Latina women—women who definitely did not fit any of the stereotypical molds found in most Hollywood films.

But the pair did not give up. They kept trying, kept knocking on doors, until they finally found a studio that was willing to take a chance. That studio was HBO, the company known for taking a chance on "risky," supposedly noncommercial projects. With HBO's backing, the producers began holding auditions, looking for girls who could believably play the role of Ana.

The problem, of course, was that most Latina actresses didn't physically match up to the role. In fact, as the film's

It was the independent film *Real Women Have Curves* that got Ferrera noticed for her phenomenal acting talents. While promoting the film, she met Salma Hayek, who would cast Ferrera in the role of Betty Suarez years later.

director, Patricia Cardoso, recounted, "We actually did an open call and put in . . . a sign that said, 'No skinny girls please.' And all these skinny girls came. But the interesting thing about it is many of them thought they were fat even though they were skinny, and I can relate to that."[7]

But when America Ferrera came in to audition, the director knew that, at least, she was physically right for the part. When she actually auditioned, though, the director was convinced that the part was hers. Not that she was immediately given the role. There were a lot of Latina actresses out there, and everybody concerned with the project knew that without the right actress to play Ana, the whole film would fall apart. Still, there was something special about America's audition, as director Patricia Cardoso remembered, "She was very smart and talented, and she was really committed to being an actress. I knew the movie depended on her."[8]

After seven callbacks, America Ferrera got the good news. The part of Ana, a smart, first-generation Mexican American finding her way and trying to make it on her own was hers. Ana, torn between her mother's traditional values and following her own dreams, was a part that America Ferrera could definitely relate to. Now all she had to do was translate those feelings onto the screen.

America relished acting in her first really big role. "I really like playing this girl because she's so confident. Her confidence is actually contagious. It's so important to show young girls that you have to be strong to survive in this world."[9] Ferrera would need every bit of Ana's confidence to act in one of the film's most powerful scenes. In it, Ana, attempting to prove a point both to herself and the other ladies in the factory, takes off her shirt and pulls down her pants to dance and compare cellulite with the other women!

Although America had done something like this many times in the privacy of her home with her sisters, it was a completely different matter doing it in front of a camera crew, knowing that it would be seen by countless others and that it would be on film forever. America's mother begged her not to do it, but Ferrera knew that the scene was an essential one in terms of the film's plot and Ana's character.

"It was very hard to do," America told *Today*. "I had to feign a lot of confidence at the time. But it's hard when it's for a camera, and it's hard when the world's going to watch it, and it's hard when there's twenty men standing around."[10] Ferrera knew that the scene was vital in terms of the film's look at the role that body image has among Latina women, a subject which Ferrera is quite familiar with, and one that she recognized was an obvious similarity between her and Ana: "The obvious parallel is the whole body image question. Ana is growing up with a generation that is so obsessed with image and having the perfect body, looking and dressing like a pop star. As an actor, you're kind of expected to submit to that and almost to lead that 'cult' almost. Getting the opportunity to counteract that was attractive."[11]

What perhaps wasn't quite as attractive were the hours Ferrera found herself working. Every morning for eight weeks, she would have to wake up at 4:00 A.M., spend 12 long hours on the set, then drive for two hours back home where she still had to do that day's schoolwork It was a grueling experience, and looking back, Ferrera still isn't quite sure how she got it all done. "It was tough. When you're in the midst of a hurricane, you don't feel the whole impact of it. You're just kind of working through it."[12]

But at the same time she was grateful to have received the part: "I got so lucky. But it was not easy. It was hard. It was my first movie, my second project ever, and I had to be in every single frame. And then I had to confront all these things that are relevant to my life. The whole image thing."[13] But if Ferrera thought making the film was like surviving a hurricane, she would be totally shocked at the media storm that began at the film's premiere.

RAVE REVIEWS

Real Women Have Curves made its debut at the 2002 Sundance Film Festival, in Park City, Utah. The festival, the largest independent film festival held in the United States, draws top actors, directors, and producers. So it was quite an honor when America Ferrera and her mother sat down in the theatre with 500 other movie professionals and watched herself on the big screen for the first time in her life.

"I was so nervous," she told Oprah Winfrey months later. "It was the most surreal thing I've ever experienced in my life."[14] And one of the most gratifying. At the end of the film, much to America's shock and surprise, the entire audience stood up and cheered. In her first starring role, America Ferrera had earned a standing ovation from an audience of her peers!

She received far more than a standing ovation. *Real Women Have Curves* received the Audience Award at that year's Sundance Film Festival. And America received the Jury Award for Best Actress. More awards followed, as Ferrera received nominations for an Independent Spirit Award for Best Debut Performance and for the Young Artist Award for Best Performance by a Leading Young Actress.

Her reviews were laudatory, or praiseworthy. Writing for the *Chicago Sun-Times*, Pulitzer Prize–winning film critic Roger Ebert wrote of her performance that,

> Ferrera is a wonder: natural, unfocused, sweet, passionate and always real . . . for young women depressed because they don't look like skinny models, this film is a breath of common sense and fresh air. *Real Women Have Curves* is a reminder of how rarely the women in the movies are real . . . how refreshing to see America Ferrera light up the room with a smile from the heart.[15]

And writing in *Variety*, the movie industry newspaper, David Rooney added that,

> Relative newcomer Ferrera . . . is remarkable, her sensitive perf[ormance] revealing the internally battling forces of strength, resolve, defiance, duty and loyalty that shape and color her character.[16]

It was a star-making performance. It was a movie that challenged clichés and stereotypes, while exploring the issues of body image and weight that women of every age and ethnic group could easily relate to. As America bravely asked on the *Today* show, "When was the last [time] that the ingénue of the film was over a size four?"[17]

But what made the film resonate with viewers was that although the cast and roles were Latina, they didn't really have to be. "You can replace that with whatever—black, white, Asians," said America. "It's the same story because it's about things we all face."[18] That resonance, the universality of the story led HBO to make an important and unexpected decision. The film had originally been made to be shown strictly on television. But given the nerve that the film struck, and the remarkable reviews garnered by the film and its cast, the network decided to release the film to be shown in movie theaters nationwide.

When *Real Women Have Curves* opened on October 18, 2002, in theaters in Los Angeles, San Francisco, and New York, America Ferrera found herself the young star that everybody wanted to interview. She even found herself being interviewed by the "Queen of Daytime Television" herself, Oprah Winfrey, appearing as part of a December program about movies that people should see. It was a big moment for Ferrera, and one that years later would pay dividends in unexpected ways. For it was on this show that America Ferrera met Salma Hayek, who would remember the young star when the time came to cast a new television show entitled *Ugly Betty*.

But when the hubbub from *Real Women Have Curves* finally died down, America Ferrera found herself back in nearly the same position she had been in before the movie premiered. As a Latina actress, and one with curves, roles were still not easy to come by. And, like every other young actress, Ferrera found herself, despite her newfound fame, facing round after round of auditions after auditions. But with roles in movies limited, Ferrera found herself switching her focus, and she began finding challenging dramatic roles on television.

STRETCHING HER TALENTS

All the time she was working on her career, she was also continuing her education. She had filmed *Real Women Have Curves* during her senior year in high school. And now, like Ana, she had a decision to make: Should she go on to college (she graduated number one in her high school class) despite her big-screen success and make her mother happy, or should she pursue her career full-time?

She ended up doing both. Although she had already been accepted by the University of Southern California (USC), where she planned to major in international relations, she put her first year in college off for one semester to be part of the publicity for *Real Curves* and "because I wanted my life outside of acting to be, you know, a life."[19] Yet, as she said in an interview, "Acting is something I knew I wanted to do long-term.

THE SUNDANCE FILM FESTIVAL

From its simple beginnings as the Utah/US Film Festival, the Sundance Film Festival has emerged as the largest independent cinema festival in the United States and the premier showcase for new works from American and international independent filmmakers.

Many of today's most important directors got their big break at Sundance, including Kevin Smith (*Clerks*), Robert Rodriguez (*Spy Kids*), Quentin Tarantino (*Pulp Fiction*), and Steven Soderburgh (*Erin Brockovich*). The festival has also served as a launching ground for some of the biggest independent film hits of recent years: *The Blair Witch Project*, *Little Miss Sunshine*, *Napoleon Dynamite*, and even 2009's Academy Award nominee *Precious*. For young aspiring filmmakers, getting their film shown here can be the beginnings of a great career.

But not going to college was not an option. I think it probably helped me as an actress as well, because actresses need real-life experiences as well."[20]

Still, when she entered college in the spring semester of 2002, despite being her class valedictorian with a G.P.A. (grade point average) of 4.4, despite the respect she had earned for her performance in *Real Women*, she still felt the same sense of intimidation, of nerves, of being afraid she wouldn't fit in, as does nearly every other college freshman. She told the school newspaper, *The Daily Trojan*, "When I came here as a freshman, I was so moved and so in awe of how uninformed I was."[21]

Despite her sense of awe, she went to work with the same sense of determination as she did in her acting career. She took a double major in theater and international relations Why international relations? "I was amazed at how ignorant Americans are of the world outside this country. I don't want to be one of those," she told FilmMonthly.com.[22] In addition, she saw how studying international relations could help her acting career. "Film and media are such a huge part of political culture," she told her school newspaper. "My education will not only always be with me, but will always be a part of the work I do."[23]

Being a full-time student didn't mean that she had abandoned her dream of being an actress. Far from it. Her schedule, though, meant that she had to restrict the roles she took to those she could do during breaks or during vacation. But despite the recognition she received for *Real Women Have Curves*, good parts didn't always come easily. Her first role after *Real Women* was as a high school student suffering from obsessive compulsive disorder (OCD) on the hit CBS television series *Touched by an Angel*, which aired on October 19, 2002.

The character that Ferrera played, Charlee, was an OCD sufferer whose disorder caused her to worry constantly about virtually every aspect of her life—checking her locker constantly to make sure it was locked, for example. Charlee worries so much about everything that during class she begins

Ferrera's performance in *Real Women Have Curves* earned her the Special Jury Prize for Acting at the prestigious Sundance Film Festival. In this photo, she makes her acceptance speech.

to believe that the air is dirty and begins to have problems breathing. Fortunately, with the help of the series star, Roma Downey, who plays an angel who comes to earth to help people with their problems, Charlee's problems are solved by the end of the episode.

While the show itself may have seemed slightly contrived, the role of Charlee gave Ferrera a chance to test her acting chops on a kind of role she had never played before. And she passed the test with flying colors. CBS was so pleased with her performance that they offered her a role in the Hallmark Hall of Fame production of *Plainsong*, a made-for-TV movie about life in a small town in rural Colorado, based on the popular novel of the same name by Kent Haruf.

In the film, Ferrera played what is often a cliché role— an unmarried teen mother—but in this case one who, after her alcoholic mother forces her to leave the house, moves in with two bachelor brothers who give her a home and care for her. Performing with such acclaimed actors as Aidan Quinn, Rachel Griffiths, and Marion Seldes, Ferrera more than held her own, and she contributed a touching portrait of a teenager in trouble.

CBS was obviously impressed with her work and gave her yet another opportunity to stretch her wings as an actress, with a part in one of the network's biggest hit shows: *CSI: Crime Scene Investigation*.

Ferrera appeared in the episode entitled "Harvest," which first aired on October 14, 2004. In it, America plays an 18-year-old named April who reports that her younger sister, Alicia, has been kidnapped from her car by a middle-aged man. But things aren't quite what they seem, especially when the police learn that April herself is a troubled teen who has spent time in juvenile detention for intention to distribute heroin and has been kicked out of her home by her parents.

Plot twist follows plot twist, and although at the end we learn that her character wasn't involved in the abduction, once again Ferrera did get the opportunity to play against "type" by portraying for the third time in a row, not the sweet, good-natured character she had portrayed in *Real Women Have Curves*, but a flawed, troubled teen.

MORE MOVIES

Along with her roles on popular television shows that served to make her known to a large viewing audience, Ferrera continued to make movies as well, albeit small "art" films. Of these, the best known is the skater and surfer film *Lords of Dogtown*, directed by Catherine Hardwicke. Based on the real-life story of the Z-Boys, a group of 1970s skaters who changed the sport of skateboarding, it is perhaps best remembered today for the performance of Heath Ledger. Ledger, while not the "star" of the film, plays Skip Engblom, who owns the Zephyr surf shop and sponsors the Z-Boys in competition, making them (and the new world of competitive skateboarding) famous.

In *Dogtown*, Ferrera played the role of legendary skater-groupie Thunder Monkey. It was an interesting part for her to play, in a movie dominated by male roles, as she said in an interview: "Catherine really wanted to put girls in the movie 'cause she thought that these girls played such a huge part in their culture. I mean, though they were like the periphery . . . chicks were just the ones on the sides—it was for the chicks that the guys did this, you know? To get the attention and to get, like, girls and whatever."[24]

The Lords of Dogtown has gone on to become a cult classic, as has another film Ferrera made around the same time, entitled *How the Garcia Girls Spent Their Summer*. America was back on more familiar territory with this film, which tells the story of three generations of Mexican-American women, each of them looking for love in their own way. America's character, Bianca, is so disappointed and unhappy with the boys in her own town that she is forced to look beyond for the boyfriend of her dreams. *The Garcia Girls*, like *Real Women*, was selected to be screened at the Sundance Festival.

REAL LIFE

Of course, along with her roles on television and in film, Ferrera's "real" life continued as well. There were books to be read and papers to be written for college. (A lot of work got done during the time between takes, when Ferrera could generally be found in her trailer, studying away.)

It was a lot to handle—working on films and television as well as studying full-time in school—but there was no way that Ferrera was going to give up or do less than her best in either part of her life. She loved acting too much, and her mother had ingrained in her too well the importance of getting an education. And, perhaps surprisingly, she took her college education as seriously as she did her acting—school was never seen as something to do "just in case" the whole acting thing didn't work out. "I've never considered falling back on anything. That's just not my philosophy in life. I don't prepare to fail. [My major] is something that I am and have always been really interested in."[25] All of which made for an interesting balancing act for Ferrera, as she went from being a star actor to just another student on campus on a regular basis. And, as if her schedule wasn't busy enough, there was still more for this tireless young actor to do.

Knowing that she had been blessed with opportunity, both by having a mother who was there for her and continuously stressed the importance of education as well as by her career, Ferrera, like many college students, felt a responsibility to give something back to the community. She regularly volunteered at a third-grade class at Norwood Street Elementary School as a Peace Games student. This program, offered by UCS College's Joint Educational Project, was designed to bring college students into elementary school classes with the goal of teaching younger students how to resolve conflicts without resorting to violence. By doing this, Ferrera hoped to do her part in stopping the spread of violence in the schools. She told the *USC College News*, "It starts on the grand scale. There are huge political powers. The 'man' and government, but it boils down to this. What makes up our society comes down to the individual and how we treat each other as individuals."[26]

Of course, the students often recognized Ferrera from her film and television roles, but she wasn't there in the role of the famous actress. She was there to help, and she took her role there very seriously. "Once you realize people are looking at you whether you like it or not, you're expected to set an example. There's a responsibility that comes along with what I do."[27] As she told *USC College News*, however, her reasons for doing volunteer work were not strictly charitable. "I do it for selfish reasons. It makes me really happy."[28]

And between her occasional acting roles, her schoolwork, her volunteer work, and her longtime boyfriend, Ryan Williams, a fellow student at USC, Ferrera *was* really happy. College life agreed with her, as she told the *Sacramento Bee*, "It's something I enjoy. I think it has a big part in the way I do everything, the roles I pick and the way I see the world and things I choose to associate myself with."[29]

Indeed, Ferrera's studies forced her to face an important question: How could acting compare in importance with what she might be able to accomplish with a degree in international relations? She told Cosmogirl.com that "when I first started college, I felt very conflicted about my passion for acting and filmmaking. I couldn't see how it could be important in a world with so much war and hatred, where people are starving to death and dying."[30]

It was one of her professors who pointed out to her that through her work as an actress she had the power to change people's lives for the better. He had been mentoring a young Latina girl, and she asked him to watch the film *Real Women Have Curves* because there, on the screen, Ferrera was portraying the emotions and feelings that she couldn't express herself. "She had always felt invisible in the world, but the movie changed her life by giving her a voice and a better understanding of herself," Ferrera confided to Cosmogirl. com. "That made me feel so much better about what I could do."[31]

Having learned firsthand the very real way her performances could touch and change people's lives reaffirmed for Ferrera that choosing acting as her career was a wise choice. Little did she realize that her next film would be her biggest hit to date, touch the lives of more young women (and men) than she could possibly imagine, and bring her one step closer to superstardom.

Breakthrough

The film was *The Sisterhood of the Traveling Pants*, **based** on the 2001 novel by Ann Brashares. The book had been a huge best seller, striking a chord with millions of readers who found it easy to relate to the story of four female friends magically linked by a pair of secondhand jeans during their first summer apart. The jeans fit them all perfectly, despite their various shapes and sizes.

Given the book's popularity, it was only a matter of time before it was made into a movie. Casting the four female leads was of vital importance—fans of the book had such strong feelings and opinions about each of the characters that without the right cast those same fans would stay away from theaters in droves.

Actress Amber Tamblyn, known then for her starring role in the television series *Joan of Arcadia*, was cast in the role of Tibby, the tough wannabe filmmaker who is forced to spend the summer at home babysitting while her friends get to spend the summer traveling. Alexis Bledel, beloved for her role as Rory Gilmore on the TV series *Gilmore Girls*, was awarded the part of Lena, the sheltered yet free-spirited teen who spends the summer on a Greek island with her grandparents. Blake Lively, largely unknown at the time but now famous for her role as Serena van der Woodsen on *Gossip Girl*, landed the role of Bridget, who spends her summer at a soccer camp in Mexico.

The last role to be cast was that of Puerto Rican Carmen, who goes to visit her father in South Carolina and learns that he is about to remarry into a privileged white family. The role was perhaps the emotional center of the film, as well as the film's most complex character, so careful casting of the part was essential.

The producers were interested in looking at America for the part, and her agent sent her a copy of the script, telling her that it was an interesting role and one that she should seriously consider taking. But, uninterested, Ferrera let the script sit on her desk unread. Finally, at the urging of her mother she read it and "was so amazed at what I found. It's just this story about really beautiful characters and [an] honest portrayal of being young. And it wasn't cheesy and sappy, and it wasn't any of those things. And I went in and met with the director and the producer, and then—they postponed it for an entire year. . . . But I did love the script, so I went and got the first book and read the book, loved it, then ran out and got the second book and loved it. So by that time, I was, like, a huge fan of the books, and then a year later, they called back and said, 'Okay, we're doing it now.' And by that time, I was so invested in the script and the books [that] I was like, 'Oh, I have to do this.'"[1]

With the casting set, filming could begin; but the producers and directors still had one concern. While the cast looked good on paper, nobody knew whether or not the four young, very different actresses would mesh, would work together well, and would have the personal chemistry necessary for the project to be a success.

They needn't have worried. The four young actresses not only worked together well but also quickly became fast friends, a friendship that translated into their work on the screen. As America told the *Sacramento Bee*, "We got very lucky that they put us four girls together, because we had a lot of chemistry, and we really like each other in real life, so that it made it easier to play it on-screen. When we are all four together, it's like a distinct personality. We're not really whole until we're all together."[2]

The film's director, Ken Kwapis, did what he could to encourage the feeling of friendship and camaraderie. "Most of the rehearsal process was devoted to creating opportunities for [the actresses] to bond and become friends. I came up with this odd acting exercise where I took them to a vintage clothing store and gave them two hours and seventy-five dollars apiece to buy something in character. The purpose of the exercise was not about buying something but about forming a group in the group dynamic. . . . It was really interesting. In a very natural way they found things that made their friendship feel lived-in."[3]

The team of talented actresses bonded over more than a mutual love of clothes and shopping. The message of the film was one that resonated with all four of them, as Ferrera explained to the *Sacramento Bee*. "We all know how special this project is and how lucky we are to be a part of it. I just love that it's so real and so honest. It's this portrayal of being young that we don't see so often in movies, which is that young people are just as complex and just as layered and just as strong as any other grown-up."[4]

And in Ferrera's opinion, the actresses' off-screen friendship helped to mirror one of the film's major themes: "Teenage girls are sometimes portrayed so negatively these days. Girls are competitive and backstabbing and conniving and we're always each other's enemy. This movie shows how beautiful

Mainstream movies came calling with an opportunity to play one of the leads in the movie adaptation of the popular young adult novel *The Sisterhood of the Traveling Pants*. Ferrera (with costar Amber Tamblyn in a scene from the movie) won the role of Carmen, the neglected daughter who is the emotional heart of the story.

and fulfilling and valuable those relationships can be, because we're all going through the same things in our lives, and it would be silly not to look to each other for support."[5]

America continued in her praise for the complexity of the characters in an interview: "[Brashares wrote] with so much respect for these characters. You know, she really respected the strength it took for these girls to confront growing up. And when I read it, I just really thought she had done such an amazing thing for young girls 'cause when you read the book and when you watch this movie, it gives the sense of—although you're young—you have value to your opinions, and you have a certain amount of control in your life and the choices that you make and even confronting the adults who think they may know what's right and what's best for you: that you should trust yourself in these decisions and making those choices."[6] This idea was one that had personal meaning for Ferrera, who undoubtedly remembered the conflicts she had had with own mother about her own decision to become an actress.

It was also a mutual admiration society between America Ferrera and the author of *The Sisterhood of the Traveling Pants*, Ann Brashares. Brashares said of Ferrera that "I got to see America, who is the most delightful person. She's a real reader.

$5.15/HOUR

Richard Linklater is known for being one of America's most interesting and innovative young filmmakers. Among his best-known and most successful projects are the films *Dazed and Confused*, *Before Sunrise*, *Waking Life*, *School of Rock*, *Before Sunset*, and the 2005 remake of *Bad News Bears*.

Not all of his projects have been so successful, though. In 2004, Linklater wrote and directed a pilot episode for a potential HBO sitcom called *$5.15/hour*, about the lives and adventures of a group of underpaid employees at a chain diner. Among the stars of the wannabe series? None other than America Ferrera!

HBO passed on the show, which Linklater attributed to Hollywood's lack of interest in shows about the lives of actual people working in real jobs. Linklater later used much of what he learned shooting the pilot in his 2006 film *Fast Food Nation*.

I had the galleys of the third book with me, and she started reading it right there. She's so interested and eager and so into the book: that made me feel great."[7]

A CHALLENGING CHARACTER

The role of Carmen was a challenge for America to play. While the character is very open with her friends and her mother, she shuts down with her father and acts in passive-aggressive ways with her father's new family. While basically likable, she's not always easy to get to know or to deal with. Ferrera had to confront these complexities when playing the role: "I [didn't] want people to look at this girl and say, 'My god, she's such a brat!' —She's so upset that—she's selfish, and she doesn't want her dad to be happy, and—that's hard to play and—I don't know—I think she came out lovable and complex, but I think it comes back to that idea of how well the story was created and these characters, because unlike most teenagers that we're used to seeing on TV and screen, they're portrayed as real people and have just as many layers as any 40-year-old character could have too."[8]

One aspect of the character that America could respond to on a personal level was the fact that her parents, like America's, were divorced. And by playing a character who continued to have contact with her father after the divorce, who had problems dealing with it and her father's new family, she was able to see and play out an experience very different from hers. "When my parents split up, I was very young, and that was kind of, you know—that was the end of it. I was just raised like my mom was both to me, my mother and my father, and growing up, I never understood the, like teenage angst thing about the parents being divorced, 'cause for me it was like, 'My gosh,' I couldn't even imagine having to deal with a father, too! . . . A dad who says you can't go out on dates and have people over. I couldn't even imagine! But I never had that. I never had a resentment towards him . . . And so I really loved this character Carmen, who—you know, when she goes into the summer, it's not like 'Oh my god, I have to go spend a summer with my loser father who never pays attention to me.' It's heartbreaking because she goes into it with every expectation of him fulfilling all the imaginations that she's had in her relationship with her father. And then, he falls short of it. Then he disappoints her. And I loved that. I loved that it was a young girl who was not beaten down by it: 'My parents are divorced, and that's why I'm a loser.' . . . And not to invalidate people who are, you know, deeply affected by their parents' separation, but I was so young, and so I didn't know anything else."[9] So although America Ferrera didn't go through Carmen's experiences, she was still able to imagine what it was like, to put herself into Carmen's shoes, and put *that* on the big screen. And that's why they call it acting.

Acting in the film gave her the opportunity to do other things as well. She learned to play tennis for the part. She got to sing a song from the Broadway musical *A Chorus Line*, a show she had performed in high school. And, by playing a character who has a close relationship with her mother, she got the opportunity to think about her relationship with her own mother, and to come to terms with the reasons that her mother had been opposed to her acting career: "[My mother] wanted me to go to school and be a doctor and be a lawyer . . . She never thought that my dreams of being in films would ever really come to pass and—when they did, it was very daunting for her because . . . the path that she had envisioned my life going on—completely turned around and went the other way. . . . But I think that over the years she realized that I don't want anything else out of this except to do what I love to do."[10]

Making *The Sisterhood of the Traveling Pants* was quite an experience for Ferrera. She got the opportunity to play a role she really wanted to play, using her own life experiences, imagination, and acting ability to bring the part to life. She became close friends with her fellow teen actors. And, she won the respect of the adult actors in the film as well. Bradley

The Sisterhood of the Traveling Pants was so popular that it spurred a sequel. Above, the four lead actresses, left to right: Amber Tamblyn, Blake Lively, America Ferrera, and Alexis Bledel.

Whitford, the noted actor of stage, screen, and television, perhaps best known for his Emmy Award–winning performance on the show *The West Wing*, had nothing but great things to say about Ferrera, who played his daughter in *The Sisterhood of the Traveling Pants.*

"All these girls are great in the movie, but America I adore. She is a wonderful, wonderful young actress," he said in an interview on *Today.*[11] Indeed, so impressed was Whitford with America's talents that he didn't hesitate to sign her up for one of his own personal theater projects. "I snagged her for this play I'm doing in LA. I'm directing a benefit called *Speak Truth to Power.*"[12]

But while earning the respect of her peers is important, for a movie to be successful, for Hollywood to see Ferrera as a "bankable" star, the film had to draw audiences. Many movies come and go without attracting the notice of the public. Would *The Sisterhood of the Traveling Pants*, a movie without any explosions, special effects, or major stars become a success?

It was. Fans of the book turned out to see their favorite characters brought to life by a quartet of talented actresses. Others, unfamiliar with the books, came to the film drawn by the rave reviews, many of which singled out America Ferrera for special praise. Writing for the *Boston Phoenix*, Alicia Potter called her "a standout."[13] Stella Papamichael for the *BBC* said that "Ferrera is supremely charismatic as the no-nonsense Latina."[14]

The critic for the *Fresno Bee* proclaimed that "Ferrera is especially remarkable. She transitions from comedic to tearjerking with ease, showing her full range of astounding ability."[15] Ruthe Stein, writing for the *San Francisco Chronicle* wrote that "For such a young actress, Ferrera is extraordinarily adept at expressing emotions, and she pulls out all the stops when Carmen tearfully confronts Dad with her fears."[16] Alison Benedkit, writing in the *Chicago Tribune* promised her readers that "Ferrera is the star of the show, no doubt about that."[17]

But it was *The New Zealand Press* that perhaps summed it up best, praising the entire cast, but going on to say that "The standout performance, however, would have to be America Ferrera, who brings a palpable realness to her role."[18]

The reviews were all that Ferrera could have hoped for and then some. The movie was a huge hit, earning close to $40 million in the United States alone. By a wild coincidence, Ferrera's other film, *Lords of Dogtown,* hit the big screen at the same time as *The Sisterhood of the Traveling Pants.*

It was quite the combination for Ferrera—one mainstream box office hit and one independent "art" film, both of which showed off her undeniable talent and range as an actor. And her work had not gone unnoticed. She received both the Imagen Foundation Award for Best Actress, given for positive portrayals of Latinos in the entertainment industry, as well as the Movieline Breakthrough Award.

It had been a big year careerwise for Ferrera, but she was not content to rest on her laurels. While most young actresses would strike while the career iron was hot and try to continue their big-screen success, America took a different route. Instead of appearing in a movie seen by millions, she opted to test herself in the theater, playing to audiences of less than 300 people each night. Instead of trying to remake herself into the thin girl of Hollywood's dreams, she used her own beauty to help redefine what beauty is. And, because of all these factors and more, she was about to be offered the biggest role of her career to date.

Becoming
a Star

So, in December of 2005, instead of America Ferrera taking a well-deserved rest and enjoying the Southern California sun, she made her New York stage debut at the Century Theatre for the Performing Arts, in the play *Dog Sees God: Confessions of a Teenage Blockhead.*

An unauthorized parody of the popular *Peanuts* comic strip, the play imagines what its characters would be like as teenagers. Ferrera played the role of Charlie Brown's sister. (In the play, since it was an unauthorized use of Charles Schultz's well-loved characters, Charlie Brown is called simply "CB" and his sister, who in the comics is named Sally, is called "CB's sister." Given the fact that the play opens with CB and his sister holding a funeral for their dog who had just died of rabies, it's no wonder that the show was unauthorized.)

The show was a huge hit (in off-Broadway terms), winning, among other awards, Theatermania's Play Award, the

GLAAD Media Award for Best Off-Off Broadway Production, and Broadway.com's 2006 Audience Award for Favorite Off-Broadway Production. (Television fans who made their way to the Century Theatre to see the play got an additional treat besides seeing America Ferrera—also in the cast were Eliza Dushku, known for her work on *Buffy the Vampire Slayer*, *Angel*, and *Dollhouse*, and Ian Somerhalder, known for his roles on *Lost* and *The Vampire Diaries*.)

Of course, Ferrera wasn't content just to be acting in a hit play night after night. She was also earning college credits by taking classes at New York University. And, if that wasn't enough, she also became a spokesperson for the Dove Campaign for Real Beauty, a series of advertisements for Dove products featuring "real" people without the usual model-like figures and attitudes.

Ferrera was pleased that she had been selected for the campaign, hoping that it would prove to other young women that beauty comes in many shapes and sizes, and that the usual standard for beauty portrayed in the media is not the only one. "I hope young girls understand the manufactured images around them," Ferrera said, speaking out about the typical ad campaign featuring picture-perfect models with nearly unattainable looks and figures. "It's those people's job to look like that."[1]

There is, of course, an irony to the fact that America Ferrera was appearing in a nationwide ad campaign extolling her natural beauty, because she was about to get offered the role that would force her to hide that beauty, and to become a character known for her distinct *lack* of beauty.

SHOULD SHE TAKE IT?

Once Salma Hayek finally got the green light by ABC Television to produce an American version of the Colombian telenovela *Betty La Fea*, there was only one actress she had in mind to play the title role of Betty Suarez—America Ferrera. And why not? With stage, television, and film experience, and the seeming ability to take any role and make it her own, Ferrera was the obvious choice. But would she take the part?

The answer wasn't quite as obvious as it seems today from the perspective of the show's success. Ferrera's career in film was really just taking off. If she took the role and went to work starring in a television series, movies as well as theater would have to be largely put aside, scheduled only during breaks in filming the show. And then of course there's always the other question: After making a name for yourself in movies, is a starring television role as prestigious as a film role? As she said in an interview with w.magazine.com, "Honestly, I never saw myself doing TV."[2]

But all of her questions and worries evaporated after just a few meetings with one of her idols, Salma Hayek. "Salma was so convincing. Salma is the kind of person who could sell you, like, a used stereo. She promised me that it would be done in the right way, and I trusted her."[3]

"SMILES FOR SUCCESS"

Along with a busy schedule acting and studying, Ferrera is also a young woman who believes in giving back to the community. Ferrera is a proud sponsor of Smiles for Success. This foundation was established in 1995 by members of the American Association of Women Dentists (AAWD).

As it states on their Web site, Smiles for Success was formed to assist women who are moving from welfare to work and cannot afford the cost of dental care. These are women who, perhaps for years, have been unable to afford to go the dentist, so now, facing job interviews for the first time, they may be self-conscious, embarrassed, or even in pain as they attempt to hide decayed, missing, and damaged teeth.

Smiles for Success repairs their teeth and some of their self-esteem, which can help them on the road to getting a job so that they can support both themselves and their families.

Of course, it took more than Hayek's charm and promises to get Ferrera to take the part. As we've seen, America, despite her young age, was determined not to take just any role. She would only take parts that were meaningful to her, would present her with a challenge as an actor, and not be a stereotypical Latina role. "When they explained the character to me, they had already fallen in love with her, and I fell in love with her."[4]

There was more to Ferrera's feelings of love for Betty that compelled her to accept the part—it was also a role that struck a nerve with her, and one that she hoped would strike the same nerve with audiences: "As soon as Salma showed me the script, I knew it mirrored some of the insecurities I had—and still have. There's a vulnerable nakedness to Betty. She's an awkward young woman determined to succeed in a world which seems as though it has been specifically designed for hip people only. I think audiences look at her and say, 'I can recognize my own clumsiness, my own awkwardness, my own insecurity there.' There are times you feel sexy and confident and there are times you feel like Betty."[5]

THE MAKING OF UGLY BETTY

Once Ferrera accepted the part, the show's producers, writers, and designers all went to work, not only to adapt *Yo soy Betty, la fea* to its new United States setting, but also to build the role to take advantage of Ferrera's strengths as an actress.

The show would be placed in the high-powered, fast-paced world of a Manhattan-based fashion magazine called *Mode*. By way of contrast, Betty's home life would be set in a decidedly non-high-powered, non-fast-paced working-class neighborhood in the borough of Queens, where Betty, despite her glamorous working life in Manhattan, would still be living with her father, sister, and nephew.

Establishing the contact between the two very different worlds—the fashion world of Manhattan and the "real"

Ferrera was offered the title role in the new television show *Ugly Betty*, but she never could have imagined the show would become as popular as it did. Although Ferrera was concerned about accepting a role in a television series just as her film career was taking off, the opportunity to play a character like Betty Suarez convinced her it was the right thing to do.

world of Queens—was a deliberate decision on the part of the show's creator and executive producer, Silvio Horta. "In order to have the heightened fun of the fashion world, you need to ground it in something. You needed to see where Betty lives."[6]

Not only was it necessary to see where Betty lives, but for Ferrera to get a handle on the part it was important for her to figure out who Betty was and who Betty wanted to be. And the more she studied the script and analyzed her character, the more she saw herself in Betty. "Her dream is to write for magazines—not necessarily a fashion magazine, but that's where she gets a job. She has to strive even harder to show her talents because she works in a place where everyone is overly concerned with what people look like. The entertainment industry is very similar. Because I don't look like a typical glamorous Hollywood star, it was hard for me to get in the right doors. People here think they can look at you and judge what you are capable of doing. Betty and I are similar in that respect."[7]

By using her own life and personal experiences, by taking Betty's issues and making them her own, Ferrera would have what she needed to play the role, as she told Northjersey.com: "Approaching the role from a very personal way is the only way to do it. To relieve those moments that are very embarrassing and very isolating and very cold are, in a big way, heartbreaking. To make those moments real for myself, I have to draw from myself."[8]

And while Ferrera continued to dig into the character of Betty Suarez, producers went to work casting the rest of the parts. It's a tricky thing to do, since each actor has to be able to mesh together seamlessly with each of the other actors, so that the cast works together as a whole.

Eric Mabius, best known for his role in the award-winning independent film *Welcome to the DollHouse*, was given the role of Betty's boss, Daniel Meade. Becki Newton was asked to play Amanda, the sassy office secretary. Michael Urie won the role of Marc, who, along with his close ally, Amanda, enjoys nothing more than sucking up to the boss and playing practical jokes on Betty.

Ashley Jensen got the role of Christina, another of the "uglies" at the magazine and one of Betty's closest work friends. Betty's father would be played by Tony Plana, a show business professional who had appeared in over 60 films along with such hit television roles as *24* and *The West Wing*.

But undoubtedly the biggest name in the cast (even bigger than that of America Ferrera) was Vanessa Williams, a one-time Miss America who went on to a career in show business that included Broadway, television, and music, and receiving Tony, Grammy, and Emmy nominations every step of the way. She was given the plum role of conceited, self-absorbed former supermodel Wilhelmina Slater, who lives for just two things: *Mode* magazine and regular Botox injections.

The show's supreme villain, she serves as an the over-the-top ego run wild, as opposed to the show's moral center, Betty Suarez. And while some actors might be afraid of playing such an evil character, Williams had no such compunction: "They needed somebody who could pack a punch, who would be a formidable foe for setting up the drama. It's an honor to play somebody who is so strong. Of course she is evil and demonic and looking for the worst, but those are really fun roles to play."[9]

THE UGLIFICATION OF BETTY

As the time to begin taping the show grew closer, work began to find the right "look" —makeup, wardrobe, etc.—for the cast who would be playing the employees of a glamorous fashion magazine. Obviously, they would all be made up and dressed to look their very best, in the hippest most fashionable clothes imaginable.

But for Ferrera's role, that of fish-out-of-water Betty Suarez, the behind-the-scenes technicians had just the opposite task: They had to perform an act of "reverse glamorization"—turning the stylish and beautiful America Ferrera into the fashion-inept Betty. It was quite the challenge, as executive producer Silvio Horta told *USA Today*. "The essence is transforming this girl who is adorable and cute into a character called Ugly Betty. It requires work on wardrobe and hair and makeup (to create) these things we ascribe to being ugly."[10]

Part of the responsibility for the transformation fell to hair department head Roddy Slayton, who explained to *USA Today* the difficulties of turning America into Betty: "She's a gorgeous girl with an incredible style sensibility in her personal life. What we do is Bettify her in the morning. It's in contrast with the rest of the show, where everybody else is glammed up."[11] (Incidentally, it was Ferrera herself who came up with the word *Bettify* to explain the process of turning the glamorous Ferrera into the decidedly non-glamorous Betty.)

How did they do it? Part of it was through her wardrobe. "It's a hard character to do," said Eduardo Castro, one of the show's costume designers. "She can't be totally dumpy. She has to have some dignity to the way she dresses."[12] But by searching through nearly every vintage clothing store in New York City, Castro found what he needed: an assortment of heavy skirts, blouses, and thick eyeglasses that give Betty the innocent and schlumpy look that defines her.

Along with the wardrobe came all the rest. The bangs. The bushy eyebrows. "Unruly eyebrows is the opposite of glamour," stylist Beverly Jo Pryor told the *New York Times*.[13] Finally, a mouth full of shiny braces completed the picture. The physical look of Betty Suarez was in place.

Looking at it from the outside, it must be easy to imagine America Ferrera's dismay at looking at herself in the mirror for the first time in full-Betty regalia. After all, she was an actress and a gorgeous young woman who, like most people, wanted to look her best. But as an actress, getting into Betty's "skin" was necessary for her to finish the puzzle of who Betty was. "It's important for me to be able to feel like that character. Until I put on the right outfit, wore the right glasses, and chose the right hair, I couldn't feel like Betty."[14]

Betty Suarez struck a chord in millions across the United States. The character's mix of intelligence, competence, loyalty, determination, vulnerability, and lack of vanity was incredibly appealing, and Betty's unique personal style endeared her to everyone who had ever felt insecure.

As she told *USA Today,* by going through the physical transformation necessary to play Betty, it made it easier for her as an actress to go far with the character. "As an actor, it's almost easier to go really far when I'm in a costume, when it's somebody who's not me, because (Betty) goes through some pretty embarrassing and heartbreaking scenes. That isn't easy for me as a person, but to hide behind her mask was easier."[15]

Which is not to say that changing from America to Betty was easy for the young actress. When taping for the show first began, it took hours in hair and makeup to complete the transformation. (Eventually, the process got down to "just" an hour.) The wardrobe itself consisted of clothing that Ferrera herself would never wear. "Betty wears a lot of tights, parkas, and all these shirts buttoned up to her neck. That drives me insane. I don't like to feel restricted."[16]

Ferrera gained greater insight into the world of Betty Suarez after being "Bettified." People, it seemed, treated her different simply because she looked different: "It wasn't that people were rude. It was like I didn't exist. . . . At a newsstand, I was in line four times before I plucked up the courage to edge forward, shove my money in the guy's face, and say, 'Excuse me, but I was here first.'"[17]

But while the reactions she got in public while being "Betty" might have been discomforting, it served both to bring her closer to the character as well as to strengthen her belief that playing Betty would serve not only to empower other young women but herself as well. It took time, but, as she told *The Sun,* "When I'm wearing Betty's costume I never felt more confident and more beautiful. To me, Betty is an opportunity to represent a generation of young women who don't recognize themselves on anything they are watching."[18]

As production on the show continued, Ferrera, along with the rest of the cast, began to realize the impact their

7

The Ups and Downs of Fame

ABC's confidence in the show turned out to be completely justified. Its premiere episode, first shown on September 28, 2006, was a huge hit, with 16.3 million viewers tuning in to see just who Ugly Betty was. And what they saw they liked.

While network executives were worried that audiences might not embrace a show with such an off-putting title, they failed to consider the simple fact that the country is, in fact, filled with "Ugly Bettys"—women (or men for that matter) who for whatever reason feel they don't fit in to the world around them. In many ways, virtually everybody is an Ugly Betty.

The ratings held up as the season progressed, making it one of the season's top-rated new series. It was, in fact, the only new series to make the top 20 of the all-important Nielsen Ratings for the season, and the number-one new show in total viewers.

The show's immediate success seemed to take everybody involved by surprise. (With the possible exception of Salma Hayek, who was always supremely confident that the show would find an audience. "It's human nature," she told *ABC News*. "Human conflict, human drama, translates everywhere in the world.")[1]

Ferrera had her own theory on why the show was so popular, telling *USA Today* "What I think is successful is it's not about stereotypes. They're not hitting piñatas every weekend. More important than having Latinos on TV is having a representation of the variations of what Latino is."[2]

Indeed, for Latina women across the country, *Ugly Betty* was a breakthrough. She was a character they could relate to, a real girl in the real world, facing the problems they faced every day—those of being a first-generation Latino trying to make their way in a non-Latino society. "Her persona, in terms of

ON ACCEPTING ROLES

Throughout her career, America Ferrera has made it a rule not to just accept any role: It has to be one that allows her to express her values, to allow her to have a positive effect on her audience. Betty Suarez is no exception to that rule.

"It's so reassuring to have a woman heroine who triumphs with more than just what she has on the outside . . . who has more to offer the world than just a pretty picture. To me, the tragedy about this whole image-obsessed society is that young girls get so caught up in just achieving that they forget to realize they have so much more to offer the world."*

By taking roles such as Betty Suarez, Ferrera is able to show, far more powerfully than with just words, that beauty such as Betty's comes from within and is not dependent on glamour, style, or the latest look.

*Sheila Anderson, *America Ferrera: Latina Superstar*. Berkley Heights, N.J.: Enslow Publisher, Inc., 2009, p. 38.

personality, is what Latinas strive to be every day," one die-hard fan, Ana Pereira, told the *Boston Globe*. "You want to be a hard worker and be successful and go into any profession you want."[3]

Reactions like that, from Latinos happy to see themselves fully represented on television as real people, brought Ferrera a great deal of satisfaction. But she was quick to point out that it wasn't only Latinas who could see themselves in Betty. "This character is a very positive portrayal for young women, for Latino women, who aspire to a certain kind of dream," Ferrera explained to *USA Today*. "But you don't have to be anything like Betty to derive an attachment to the character."[4]

Indeed, given the show's immediate popularity, it was obvious that Betty struck a chord with more than just Latinas. The media pronounced the show a phenomenon and the season's best new comedy. The character was spoofed on *Saturday Night Live*—a sure sign of success. And that Halloween, trick-or-treaters across the country took to the streets, dressed up like their favorite TV character, much to Ferrera's amusement. "That was really fun to see little girls and old men dressing up as Ugly Betty."

Naturally, when executives at ABC saw the reaction to *Ugly Betty*, they decided to capitalize on it. Playing into the show's theme, they launched a public service campaign called "Be Ugly '07." Aimed at the show's core audience, it was designed to promote self-esteem among women by presenting a positive self-image and ending the destructive stereotyping of what "beauty" is. By using Betty Suarez as an example, it aimed to show women that they can be themselves, be confident, and feel beautiful without changing their looks to meet some unreachable ideal of what beauty is.

The campaign also had the support of Girls Inc., a nonprofit group that promotes programs to help young women be strong and smart. In an interview in *USA Today*, the group's president, Joyce Roche, said that the campaign "allows us to counter the message girls get that they've got to be perfect, be a certain size, look a certain way. We hope that people go beyond the headline of ugly. I wish there would have been another way of saying it, but at least it will get the dialogue going."[5]

The reaction to the show, from fans and critics, as well as the impact that the show was having on the lives of young women, was more than they could have hoped for. But the show's success continued to grow. *Ugly Betty* began showing on British television in January of 2007, and since then, it's been sold to more than 70 countries worldwide. And to make the show's popularity all the sweeter, many of those countries already had their *own* version of the original Colombian tele-novela *Yo soy Betty, la fea* on the air.

AWARD SEASON

As the award season for the 2007 television season began, *Ugly Betty*, and especially its star, America Ferrera, were right in the midst of it all.

The show won Best New Series from the Family Television Awards and Best Television Series from the Satellite Awards. It received nominations from the NAACP Image Awards, the Writers Guild Awards, and the People's Choice Awards. And when the nominations for the Golden Globes, presented by the Hollywood Foreign Press, were announced, America Ferrera found herself nominated for one of the major awards: Best Performance by an Actress in a Television Series (Musical or Comedy).

Like most of the nominees, she was awakened by an early morning call with the news. Interviewed moments later, all she could say was "It's wonderful." Fortunately, she had time to process the news and come up with some other words before the awards ceremony was held on January 15, 2007.

IMPORTANT INFLUENCES

A child of Honduran immigrants, a Latina actress whose roles have helped to redefine the role of Hispanics in film and television, America Ferrera's entire life has been influenced by the Hispanics around her.

The biggest influence, of course, was her mother, America, who, although initially unhappy about her daughter's choice of career, gave her the opportunity to follow her dream while still insisting that she continue her education and go on to college. As she said accepting her Golden Globe Award in 2007, "Everything that I've ever accomplished in this life has been due to the strength and intelligence and will you gave to me, Mommy."[*]

Her professional life as well has been both influenced and pushed forward by a talented group of Hispanic directors, playwrights, and actors. She got her big break in the film *Real Women Have Curves*, based on the play by Mexican-American Josefina Lopez. She costarred with the phenomenal Lupe Ontiveros, who played her mother, Carmen. Ontiveros had played the role of Carmen on stage as well, and inspired Ferrera not only through her performance in the film but through her career as well, as one of the founding members of Los Angeles' Latino Theatre Company.

And, of course, it's thanks to Salma Hayek, an actress whose work both as an actress and producer of films about the Latino experience have long served to inspire Ferrera, that she got the role that made her a star—Betty Suarez in *Ugly Betty*.

---

[*]Sheila Anderson, *America Ferrera: Latina Superstar*. Berkeley Heights, N.J.: Enslow Publishers, Inc., 2009, p. 37.

It was a great night for Ferrera and the show. *Ugly Betty* was named best TV comedy, vying against some stiff competition: *Desperate Housewives*, *Entourage*, *The Office*, and *Weeds*. Accepting the award was the creator and executive producer, who, surrounded by the entire cast and crew, had

In its first year on the air, *Ugly Betty* received several awards and nominations. Perhaps the highlight of the award season was the 2007 Golden Globes, at which the show won for best TV comedy and Ferrera won for best actress in a comedy. Here, the cast celebrates their award, with Ferrera and Hayek taking center stage.

this to say: "Like a lot of its characters and a lot of us up here right now, this show is an immigrant, and Betty is a testament to the American dream."[6] The dream though, was far from complete.

Shortly thereafter, it was time to announce the winner in Ferrera's category. The only first-time nominee among the group, she, too, was facing some extraordinarily tough competition: Marcia Cross and Felicity Huffman, both from *Desperate Housewives*, Julia-Louis Dreyfus, from *The New Adventures of Old Christine*, and Mary-Louise Parker from *Weeds*.

One can only imagine the flood of emotions, thoughts, and memories going through her head when actors John Stamos and Jennifer Love Hewitt opened the envelope and announced that America Ferrera was the winner. Her speech, given in a flood of tears, was a memorable one: "It is such an honor to play a role that I hear from young girls, on a daily basis, how it makes them feel worthy and lovable, and that they have more to offer the world than they thought."[7] She wasn't the only one crying. Other stars in the audience also found themselves crying at Ferrera's honest and emotional response to her win. Salma Hayek was seen weeping. ("She was crying before the award even started."[8])

Why the tears? A blogger wrote, "I think the reason why so many people love this show, this character, and this actress is that while it is a bit surreal in its presentation, it's not another cookie cutter cookie up there. It's a girl that really isn't ugly, but because she doesn't fit the ideal mold of a so-called 'perfect' woman of society today, she's somehow deemed so. The refreshing thing about this character is that she doesn't fit the other stereotype either—mousey quiet girl. So many characters who have glasses and brown hair (fashion suicide apparently) are considered to be silent doormats only interested in science. Not Betty—she speaks her mind, cherishes chic, and relentlessly pursues her dreams. . . . In

Representative Hilda L. Solis (D-California) presents America Ferrera with a copy of a resolution that applauds her for raising the profile of Latinos in popular culture and breaking down barriers in prime-time television. The congresswoman introduced the resolution to the floor of the U.S. House of Representatives on January 17, 2007.

a nutshell, Betty is a character that all women can relate to in some way, and that makes her great."[9] And in a nutshell, the same thing can be said about the actress who plays Betty, America Ferrera.

Ferrera's whirlwind award season didn't stop with the Golden Globes. She also received the Screen Actors Guild (SAG) Award for Outstanding Performance by a Female Actor in a Television Comedy Series, 2006, and to top it off, she also received the Primetime Emmy for Outstanding Lead Actress in a Comedy Series, becoming the first actress in history to win all three major acting awards in the same year.

Receiving her Emmy, she gave yet another moving speech, saying in part, "It's truly an amazing and wonderful thing that happens when your dreams come true, and I just wish that for everybody, that they get to do what inspired them."[10]

Not only did America Ferrera get to follow her dreams and get to do what inspired her, but through her work as an actress, she inspired others to follow their dreams. And it was because of this that she received one more honor in 2007: She was lauded in Congress.

Congresswoman Hilda L. Solis (D-California) took to the floor of the U.S. House of Representatives on Wednesday, January 17, two days after Ferrera's win at the Golden Globes, to honor Ferrera for her role in raising and changing the profile of Latinos in popular culture.

Madame Speaker, I rise today to congratulate America Ferrera for winning the Golden Globe for best actress in a comedy for her work in the ABC show *Ugly Betty*. Through her work, Ms. Ferrera is breaking down barriers for Latinos in prime-time television . . . I commend America and everyone involved in *Ugly Betty* for helping to break down stereotypes and provide a role model for young Latinas.[11]

Any way you look at it, it had been an extraordinary year for America Ferrera. She had gone from being a little-known actress to the star of a hit prime-time television show, the winner of every major acting award for her work, and had been praised on the floor of Congress. And she was only 24 years old. Her career was just beginning.

Being America

Even though in 2007 America Ferrera seemed to be winning every award and honor imaginable, including being named one of *Time* magazine's Top 100 Most Influential People in the World, that didn't slow the ambitious young actress down one little bit.

She spent that summer filming the sequel to *The Sisterhood of the Traveling Pants*. Ferrera enjoyed filming with the friends she'd made on the original movie. *The Sisterhood of the Traveling Pants 2* opened to good reviews and solid box-office success, as fans returned to theaters, eager to see what new adventures awaited their four heroines.

And, once again, it was Ferrera's performance that caught the attention of critics. One Associated Press review said, "America Ferrera pretty much steals the whole movie out from under her co-stars . . . Ferrera is an actress with a likable, accessible presence who always makes her performance look effortless . . . her charms only seem to strengthen as she grows older and more seasoned."[1]

THE PRICE OF FAME

With her newfound fame came fans' interest in her every move. And with fans' interest came the scourge of most celebrities—the paparazzi, photographers who stalk stars' every move, hoping to get a picture of a star in an embarrassing (or glamorous) moment that they can then sell to a magazine or tabloid.

At first, such attention can, naturally, be flattering—who doesn't like to be noticed or to have their photo taken? Achieving fame is, of course, just one of the many reasons that people enter show business. But after a while, the constant hounding of photographers and videographers can be wearying. But fortunately for Ferrera, her experiences, at

AMERICA FERRERA AND BETTE MIDLER

Although America Ferrera has spoken proudly of the long list of Latino actors and actresses whom she admires, actors whose success made hers possible, it may surprise you to know that one of her favorite stars of all time is Bette Midler.

In fact, she told the show-business "bible" *Variety* that Midler is the reason she wanted to become an actress, and that when Midler's version of the Broadway musical *Gypsy* ran on television when Ferrera was just 10 years old, she watched it as many times as she could.

Her love for Midler still holds strong today. Appearing on the *Rachael Ray Show* in October of 2008, Ferrera admitted to Ray that the dream guest she'd love to get on *Ugly Betty* was, in fact, Bette Midler. Ray then surprised America with a note from Midler herself, announcing that a tree had been planted in honor of Ferrera through Midler's Million Trees NYC initiative.

America Ferrera has used her fame to bring awareness to important causes. In the photo above, she and her sister (*far left*) bead bracelets to support cervical cancer education. She also is an ambassador for Save the Children, a charity committed to educating children around the world.

least to date, have been unexceptional, if only because she lives such a normal life. She still remembers the first time she was followed by a photographer: "I was in New York City doing *The View* with Salma Hayek; it was the day *Ugly Betty* premiered. After the show I got chased by a paparazzo on a motorcycle for an hour. I remember thinking, 'Oh my God, this is crazy, they already care about me!' When I finally got out of the car, the paparazzo yelled, 'I thought I was following Salma Hayek!' I thought, OK—that puts things into perspective."[2]

But even now, when the paparazzi know who Ferrera is, there isn't anything really exciting for them to photograph.

Being a workaholic, she doesn't have the time to do the all-night partying and carrying on that is guaranteed to get one on the cover of the *National Enquirer* or on tmz.com. "Paparazzi will sit outside my house to see where I'm going, and when they see it's the studio they'll be like 'This is boring,' and drive off. But you'd never catch me dancing on tables in public. I have no desire to be known for my personal life."[3]

Although Ferrera has no interest in being known for her personal life, fan interest means that the tabloids will *speculate* about her personal life if nothing else. In February 2007, for example, one gossip magazine ran the story that Ferrera and her longtime boyfriend, Ryan Piers Williams, had become engaged. His mom and her sisters saw it and called her to find out if it was, in fact, true. "I was like, 'Are you kidding? Did you not think I would tell you first?' And then I put out a statement that it wasn't true, and *that* became a whole news story. So now it's news when something doesn't happen? Like, news flash: California did not get hit by a hurricane today."[4]

But while stories like that can be amusing after the fact, Ferrera is anything but amused by the constant barrage of stories in the tabloids regarding her weight. The stories, in order to keep readers interested, are constantly changing: Sometimes she's accused of getting too fat, sometimes she's criticized for losing too much weight, with the implication that Ferrera wasn't living up to her own statements about being happy with her body as it was. Ferrera expresses frustration at such stories, explaining, "I want to be at a weight where I'm happy. There are times when I go to the gym and really try, and there are times when I just don't. I gain a pound; I lose a pound. But I think I've developed a really good sense of when I'm doing something for myself as opposed to when I'm doing something because of other people's expectations of me."[5]

ACTRESS AND ROLE MODEL

It is difficult to define the legacy for an actress still only in her twenties, an actress whose greatest roles and challenges are still ahead of her.

And yet, her impact as an actress and as a role model is unmistakable. Her acting talent and popularity have shown Hollywood that Latina actresses can both play a wide range of roles and appeal to a wide range of audiences, both Hispanic and non-Hispanic. And her belief in herself has shown a generation of young girls that beauty does come in all shapes and sizes. As one young fan wrote to her following her cover story in the February 2007 issue of *CosmoGIRL!* "You're the first person I ever saw in a magazine who looked like me."*

In her brief career, Ferrera already has achieved a sizable legacy of accomplishment and inspiration. It will be interesting to see what the next decades will bring.

---

*Grace Norwich, *America the Beautiful: An Unauthorized Biography*. New York: Price Stern Sloan, 2007, p. 8.

Of course, working long hours helps to keep one out of trouble and out of the eye of the paparazzi as well. "We have her working 24 hours a day," said Ben Silverman, one of *Ugly Betty*'s producers. "I mean, we have her working so damn hard, all she probably wants to do at the end of the day is collapse in a ball."[6] Even so, despite the long hours put in filming three seasons of *Ugly Betty*, Ferrera filled her free time, not with vacations on the coast of Italy, but with work, work, and more work. (She also filled the time finishing college and getting her degree in international relations in 2008.)

TAKING CHANCES

With a hit television show on her hands, you'd think Ferrera would have her pick of parts. Unfortunately, though, that just isn't the case. "When it comes to envisioning an actor

America Ferrera shops with her boyfriend, Ryan Piers Williams. Ferrera has commented that she leads a normal, "boring" life, hardly worthy of being followed by paparazzi.

in a role that they haven't seen them in, people in this business can be a little uncreative. . . . No one is willing to take a chance."[7]

So Ferrera, like Salma Hayek before her, was forced to take matters into her own hands: Producing her own films and starring in smaller independent films that, while not box-office smashes, allowed her to stretch and test her acting abilities to their utmost, while at the same time telling stories of the Latino experience.

In 2007, she starred in and executive-produced the short film *Muertas,* written and directed by her boyfriend, Ryan Piers Williams. It tells the story of the long series of unsolved murders in the bordertown of Juarez, Mexico. She starred in and executive-produced the bilingual independent film *Hacia la oscuridad* (*Towards Darkness)*, a thriller about a kidnapping in Colombia. She appeared in *La Misma Luna* (*Under the Same Moon)*, a critically acclaimed Spanish-language film that tells the story of a young boy living in Mexico trying to become reunited with his mother, who is living on the other side of the border in the United States.

By appearing in these films, Ferrera was not only able to play a wide variety of roles but also was able to use her fame to help them get the attention they deserved. Of course, her greatest fame from 2007 to 2010 was from her television show *Ugly Betty.* Critics continued to love the show (and America Ferrera's performance). But in the fall of 2009, ABC moved the show from Thursday nights to Friday nights, and its ratings dropped noticeably.

Fan protests forced ABC to announce that it would be moving the show from Friday nights to Wednesday nights starting in January 6, 2010, but the damage had already been done. On January 26, ABC announced that the show would be canceled at the end of the season and that its finale would air on April 14, 2010. Ironically, in an interview on ABC News just two days before the announcement, Ferrera had said that

"This season, season four, is my favorite season. We've never had lower ratings, and I've never been more proud of it. I love being the underdog."[8]

By the time *Ugly Betty* ended its television run on April 14, 2010, the title character Betty Suarez had been transformed: gone were her glasses, gone were her braces, and gone was her eager awkwardness. In their place was a confident young woman, ready to take on a new job in London and begin a new chapter in her life. And for America Ferrera, the end of the show meant it was time to put aside Betty's glasses and braces, and to begin a new phase of her life and career as well.

That career continues to go strong. In 2010 alone, she was one of the lead voice actors in one of the year's biggest hit films, *How To Train Your Dragon*, and has starred in two other films as well, *The Dry Land*, and *Our Family Wedding*. Other projects are in the works, including the possibility of an *Ugly Betty* feature film.

Defying stereotypes, taking chances, and committing herself completely to whatever role she selects, in her short career Ferrera has proven herself to be an actress of great talent and beauty, one who has changed forever what it means to be a Latina actress in Hollywood. But whatever direction her career takes, whether it's film, stage, or a return to television, one thing is certain—she will be an actress to watch.

Chronology

1984   America Georgina Ferrera is born in Los Angeles, California, on April 18.

2001   Driven to become an actor, she signs with a talent agency and begins going to auditions, often traveling by herself by bus.

2002   Gets her first major acting role when she lands a role in Disney's TV movie *Gotta Kick It Up!* which premieres in February.

        Makes her big-screen debut in *Real Women Have Curves*, winning a Special Jury Prize for Best Actress at the Sundance Film Festival.

2005   *The Sisterhood of the Traveling Pants* opens in theaters in June as does her other big-screen performance in the independent film *Lords of Dogtown*.

2006   *Ugly Betty* premieres on ABC September 28th.

1984
America Georgina Ferrera is born in Los Angeles, California, on April 18

2002
Lands a role in Disney's TV movie *Gotta Kick It Up!*; Makes her big-screen debut in *Real Women Have Curves*

1984

2005

2001
Signs with talent agency

2005
The Sisterhood of the Traveling Pants opens in theaters

2007   Wins a Golden Globe and a Screen Actor's Guild Award for her starring role on *Ugly Betty*. Graduates from the University of Southern California with a degree in international relations.

Named a top entertainer in *Time* magazine's annual list of the 100 Most Influential People in the World.

Receives an Emmy Award for Best Actress in a Comedy, becoming the first actress in history to win all three major awards in the same year.

2008   Premiere of *The Sisterhood of the Traveling Pants 2*.

2010   *The Dry Land* premieres at the Sundance Film Festival.

ABC announces the cancelation of *Ugly Betty*. The series finale is scheduled to air on April 14, 2010.

Becomes engaged to Ryan Piers Williams.

2006
Ugly Betty
premieres

2008
Premiere of *The*
Sisterhood of the
***Traveling Pants* 2**

2006

2010

2007
Wins a Golden Globe and a
Screen Actor's Guild Award for
her starring role on *Ugly Betty*;
Graduates from the University
of Southern California;
Receives an Emmy Award for
Best Actress in a Comedy

2010
Becomes
engaged to
Ryan Piers
Williams

Notes

Chapter One

1 "Telenovela." The Museum of Broadcast Communications. www.museum.tv/eotvsection.php?entrycode=telenovela.

2 Sandra Hernandez. "The ugly truth about 'Betty La Fea." Salon.com, June 1, 2001. http://www.salon.com/life/feature/2001/06/01/betty/print.html.

3 Timothy Pratt. "An ugly duckling steals Columbians' hearts; A plain-Jane soap star gives an ethics lesson to her country, known." *The Christian Science Monitor*, January 25, 2000. http://www.highbeam.com/doc/1G1-58934405.html.

4 Grace Norwich, *America the Beautiful: An Unauthorized Biography*. New York: Price Stern Sloan, 2007, p. 72.

5 Norwich, p. 73.

6 Norwich, pp. 76–77.

7 Norwich, p. 79.

Chapter Two

1 Clara Rodriguez, *Heroes, Lovers, and Others: The Story of Latinos in Hollywood*. New York: Oxford University Press, p. 3.

2 Rodriguez, p. 26.

3 Rodriguez, p. 61.

4 Rodriguez, p. 85.

5 Rodriguez, p. 111.

6 Rodriguez, p. 119.

7 Ibid.

8 Ibid.

9 Rodriguez, p. 241.

10 Rodriguez, p. 169.

11 Rodriguez, p. 211.

12 Ibid.

13 Norwich, p. 8.

14 Rodriguez, p. 213.

15 Rodriguez, p. 214.

Chapter Three

1 Norwich, p. 11.

2 Jenny Comita. "America Ferrera, Hot Betty." May 2007. http://www.wmagazine.com/celebrities/2007/05/america_ferrera?currentPage=1.

3 Norwich, p. 11.

4 Ibid.

5 Comita, p. 1.

6 Sheila Anderson, *America Ferrera: Latina Superstar*. Berkeley Heights, N.J.: Enslow Publishers, Inc., 2009, p. 9.

7 "America Ferrera's Child Anguish." *London News*. http://www.allinlondon.co.uk/news/index.php?news_id=2077.

8 Norwich, p. 12.

9 Ibid.

10 Norwich, p. 13.

11 "Groucho Reviews: Interview: America Ferrera—*The Sisterhood of the Traveling Pants*." May 27, 2005. http://www.grouchoreview.com/interviews/101.

12 Norwich, p. 14.

13 "Groucho Reviews." p. 101.

14 Paul Fischer. "It's 'Curves' Ahead for America." http://www.filmmonthly.com/Profiles/Articles/AmericaFerrara/America.Ferrara.html.

15 Comita, p. 1.

16 Norwich, p. 15.

17 Ibid.

18 "Biography of America Ferrera." *Current Biography*, September 2007. http://www.hwwilson.com/currentbio/cover_bios/cover_bio_9_07.htm.

19 Norwich, p. 16.

20 Ibid.

21 Bio., A. Ferrera.

22 Norwich, p. 17.

23 Bio., A. Ferrera.

24 Norwich, p. 17.

25 Norwich, p. 18.

26 Ibid.

27 Bio., A. Ferrera.

Chapter Four

1 Bio., A. Ferrera.

2 Ibid.
3 Ibid.
4 Norwich, pp. 19–20.
5 Norwich, p. 20.
6 Norwich, p. 23.
7 Norwich, p. 24.
8 Ibid.
9 Norwich, p. 26.
10 Norwich, p. 27.
11 Fischer.
12 Norwich, pp. 26–27
13 Bio., A. Ferrera.
14 Norwich, p. 28.
15 Roger Ebert. "Real Women Have Curves." *The Chicago Sun-Times*, October 25, 2002. http://rogerebert. suntimes.com/apps/pbcs. dll/article?AID=/20021025/ REVIEWS/210250310/1023.
16 David Rooney. "Real Women Have Curves." *Variety*, January 17, 2002. http://www.variety. com/index.asp?layout=print_ review&reviewid=VE111791677 5&categoryid=1401.
17 Norwich, p. 29.
18 Norwich, pp. 29-30.
19 Bio., A. Ferrera.
20 Comita, p. 1.
21 Norwich, p. 44.
22 Fischer.
23 Norwich, p. 45.
24 "Groucho Reviews," p. 101.
25 Norwich, p. 47.
26 Norwich, p. 48.
27 Ibid.
28 Ibid.
29 Norwich, p. 50.
30 Ibid.
31 Norwich, p. 51.

Chapter Five
1 "Groucho Reviews," p. 101.
2 Norwich, p. 58.
3 Norwich, pp. 58–59.
4 Norwich, p. 59.
5 Norwich, p. 60.
6 "Groucho Reviews," p. 101.
7 Ibid.

8 Ibid.
9 Ibid.
10 Ibid.
11 Norwich, p. 61.
12 Ibid.
13 Alicia Potter. "Review of *The Sisterhood of the Traveling Pants*." *The Boston Phoenix*, June 3–9, 2005. http://www.boston phoenix.com/boston/movies/ trailers/documents/04730896.asp.
14 Stella Papamichael. "Review of *The Sisterhood of the Traveling Pants*." August 23, 2005. http://www.bbc.co. uk/films/2005/08/16/the_ sisterhood_of_the_traveling_ pants_2005_review.shtml.
15 Norwich, p. 62.
16 Ruthe Stein. "A pair of jeans unites teen pants for a summer." *San Francisco Chronicle*, June 1, 2005. http://www.sfgate. com/cgi-bin/article.cgi?f=/ c/a/2005/06/01/DDGEGD033A1. DTL.
17 Bio., A. Ferrera.
18 Norwich, p. 62.

Chapter Six
1 Bio., A. Ferrera.
2 Comita, p. 1.
3 Ibid.
4 Norwich, p. 80.
5 Bio., A. Ferrera.
6 Norwich, p. 80.
7 Norwich, pp. 81–82.
8 Norwich, p. 87.
9 Norwich, p. 83.
10 Keveney, Bill, "It's a 'Bettification' Project," *USA Today*, October 5, 2006, http://www.usatoday.com/ life/television/news/2006-10-04- betty-transform-main_x.htm.
11 Ibid.
12 Norwich, pp. 88–89.
13 Norwich, p. 89.
14 Norwich, p. 90.
15 Keveney.
16 Norwich, p. 91.

17 Ibid.
18 Norwich, p. 92.
19 Ibid.
20 "Salma Hayek—Hayek Defends Betty." January 16, 2007. http://www.contactmusic.com/news.nsf/story/hayek-defends-ugly-betty_1019201.

Chapter Seven

1 Norwich, p. 97.
2 Norwich, p. 96.
3 Ibid.
4 Norwich, pp. 98–99.
5 Oldenburg, Ann. "The fight for female self-esteem gets pretty ugly." USA Today, December 21, 2006. http://usatoday.printthis.clickability.com/pt/cpt?action=cpt&title=The+fight+for+female+self-esteem+gets+pretty+ugly++USATODAY.com&expire=&urlID=20583933&fb=Y&url=http%3A%2F%2Fwww.usatoday.com%2Flife%2Ftelevision%2Fnews%2F2006-12-20-be-ugly_x.htm&partnerID=1663.
6 Norwich, p. 105.
7 Norwich, pp. 105–106.
8 Norwich, p. 106.
9 "America Ferrera of Ugly Betty Wins Golden Globe." http://www.associatedcontent.com/article/129041/america_ferrera_of_ugly_betty_wins.html?cat=40.
10 "America Ferrera Biography." People. www.people.com/people/america_ferrera/biography.
11 "Ugly Betty's America Ferrera Saluted in Congress." www.people.com/people/article/0,,20008892,00.html.

Chapter Eight

1 Bio., A. Ferrera.
2 Laurie Sandell. "Surprise! She's a Bombshell (and You Can Be One Too)." Glamour. September 3, 2007. http://www.glamour.com/magazine/2007/09/america-ferrera.
3 Ibid.
4 Comita, p. 1.
5 Ibid.
6 Ibid.
7 Ibid.
8 Marikar, Sheila. "'Ugly Betty' Gets the Boot, Despite America Ferrera's Endorsement." ABC News, January 27, 2010. http://blogs.abcnews.com/celebritygossip/2010/01/america-ferrera-on-best-ugly-betty-season.html.

Bibliography

Anderson, Sheila. *America Ferrera: Latina Superstar*. Berkeley Heights, N.J.: Enslow Publishers, Inc., 2009.

Comita, Jenny. "America Ferrera, Hot Betty." May 2007. Available online. URL: http://www.wmagazine.com/celebrities/2007/05/america_ferrera?currentPage=1.

Ebert, Roger. "Real Women Have Curves." *The Chicago Sun-Times*, October 25, 2002. Available online. URL: http://rogerebert.suntimes.com/apps/pbcs.dll/article?AID=/20021025/REVIEWS/210250310/1023.

Fischer, Paul. "It's 'Curves' Ahead for America." Available online. URL: http://www.filmonthly.com/Profiles/Articles/AmericaFerrera.html.

Hernandez, Sandra. "The ugly truth about 'Betty La Fea." June 1, 2001. Available online. URL: http://archive.salon.com/mwt/feature/2001/06/01/betty/index.html.

Keveney, Bill. "It's a 'Bettification' Project." *USA Today*, October 5, 2006. Available online. URL: http://www.usatoday.com/life/television/news/2006-10-04-betty-transform-main_x.htm.

Marikar, Sheila. "'Ugly Betty' Gets the Boot, Despite America Ferrera's Endorsement." ABC News, January 27, 2010. Available online. URL: http://blogs.abcnews.com/celebritygossip/2010/01/america-ferrera-on-best-ugly-betty-season.html.

Norwich, Grace. *America the Beautiful: An Unauthorized Biography*. New York: Price Stern Sloan, 2007.

Oldenburg, Ann. "The fight for female self-esteem gets pretty ugly." *USA Today*, December 21, 2006. Available online. URL: http://usatoday.printthis.clickability.com/pt/cpt?action=cpt&title=The+fight+for+female+self-esteem+gets+pretty+ugly+-+USATODAY.com&expire=&urlID=20583933&fb=Y&url=http%3A%2F%2Fwww.usatoday.com%2Flife%2Ftelevision%2Fnews%2F2006-12-20-be-ugly_x.htm&partnerID=1663.

Ortiz, Nelson. "Salma Hayek's 'Ugly Betty' to debut on ABC, Sept. 28th." Available online. URL: http://www.hispanicsurf.com/newsroom/2006/Betty_debuts_sept22_on_ABC-072006.htm.

Papamichael, Stella. "Review of *The Sisterhood of the Traveling Pants*." August 23, 2005. Available online. URL: http://www.bbc.co.uk/

films/2005/08/16/the_sisterhood_of_the_traveling_pants_2005_review.shtml.

Potter, Alicia. "Review of *The Sisterhood of the Traveling Pants*." *The Boston Phoenix*, June 3–9, 2005. Available online. URL: http://www.bostonphoenix.com/boston/movies/trailers/documents/04730896.asp.

Pratt, Timothy. "An ugly duckling steals Columbians' hearts; A plain-Jane soap star gives an ethics lesson to her country, known." *The Christian Science Monitor*, January 25, 2000. Available online. URL: http://www.highbeam.com/doc/1G1-58934405.html.

Rodriguez, Clara. *Heroes, Lovers, and Others: The Story of Latinos in Hollywood*. New York: Oxford University Press, 2008.

Rooney, David. "Real Women Have Curves." *Variety*, January 17, 2002. Available online. URL: http://www.variety.com/index.asp?layout=print_review&reviewid=VE1117916775&categoryid=1401.

Sandell, Laurie. "Surprise! She's a Bombshell (and You Can Be One Too)." *Glamour*, September 3, 2007. Available online. URL: http://www.glamour.com/magazine/2007/09/america-ferrera.

Stein, Ruthe. "A pair of jeans unites teen pants for a summer." *San Francisco Chronicle*, June 1, 2005. Available online. URL: http://www.sfgate.com/cgi-bin/article.cgi?f=/c/a/2005/06/01/DDGEGD033A1.DTL.

Villamor, Beatriz. "The Beauty of *Ugly Betty*." Available online. URL: http://www.newschool.edu/mediastudies/immediacy/09/spring/Papers/UglyBetty_BeaVillamor.pdf.

White, Kate. "America Ferrera." *Time*, May 3, 2007. Available online. URL: http://www.time.com/time/specials/2007/time100/article/0,28804,1595326_1595332_1616652,00.html.

Wolf, Buck. "For Salma Hayek, 'Ugly Betty' Is Sitting Pretty." ABC News, September 28, 2006. Available online. URL: http://abcnews.go.com/print?id=2502793.

"America Ferrera of Ugly Betty Wins Golden Globe." Available online. URL: http://www.associatedcontent.com/article/129041/america_ferrera_of_ugly_betty_wins.html?cat=40.

"Ugly Betty's America Ferrera Saluted in Congress." Available online. URL: www.people.com/people/article/0,,20008892,00.html.

"America Ferrera Interview," December 9, 2009. Available online. URL: http://www.femalefirst.co.uk/celebrity_interviews/America+Ferrera+Interview-74387.html.

"America Ferrera's child anguish." *London News*. Available online. URL: http://www.allinlondon.co.uk/news/index.php?news_id=2077.

"Telenovela." The Museum of Broadcast Communications. Available online. URL: http://www.museum.tv/eotvsection.php?entrycode=telenovela.

"Salma Hayek—Hayek Defends Betty," January 16, 2007. Available online. URL: http://www.contactmusic.com/news.nsf/story/hayek-defends-ugly-betty_1019201.

"Groucho Reviews: Interview: America Ferrera—*The Sisterhood of the Traveling Pants*," May 27, 2005. Available online. URL: http://www.grouchoreview.com/interviews/101.

"Interview with America Ferrera, star of Ugly Betty." *Kuwait Times*, February 10, 2007. Available online. URL: http://www.kuwaittimes.net/read_news.php?newsid=MjQwNTI=.

"Biography of America Ferrera." *Current Biography*, September 2007. Available online. URL: http://www.hwwilson.com/currentbio/cover_bios/cover_bio_9_07.htm.

"America Ferrera Biography." *People*. Available online. URL: http://www.people.com/people/america_ferrera/biography.

Further Reading

Declare Yourself: Speak, Connect, Act, Vote. More than 50 Celebrated Americans Tell You Why. Introduction by America Ferrera. New York: HarperCollins, 2008.

Donahue, Ann. *Ugly Betty: The Book.* New York: Hyperion, 2008.

Lopez, Josefina. *Real Women Have Curves.* Woodstock, Ill.: Dramatic Publishing, 1996.

Mendible, Myra. *From Bananas to Buttocks: The Latina Body in Popular Film and Culture.* Austin: University of Texas Press, 2007.

Picture Credits

page:

8: The Everett Collection

11: Martin Grimes, Pacificcoastnews/
Newscom

17: UNITED ARTISTS/THE KOBAL
COLLECTION

22: MIRISCH-7 ARTS/UNITED ARTISTS/
THE KOBAL COLLECTION

29: © Jamie Painter Young/Corbis

35: Jean-Paul Aussenard/WireImage/
Getty

41: LaVOO PRODUCTIONS/THE
KOBAL COLLECTION/GOODE,
NICOLA

48: Justin Kahn/WireImage/Getty Images

57: ALCON ENTERTAINMENT/WARNER
BROS./THE KOBAL COLLECTION/
PERA, DIYAH

61: ALCON ENTERTAINMENT/WARNER
BROS./THE KOBAL COLLECTION/
PERA, DIYAH

68: Ron Tom/ABC/Getty Images

72: ABC-TV/THE KOBAL COLLECTION

81: Kevin Winter/Getty Images

85: Dean Hendler/ABC/Getty Images

88: Newscom

91: Buhl Shawaf/PacificCoastNews/Newscom

Index

About the Author

Dennis Abrams is the author of numerous titles for Chelsea House, including biographies of Barbara Park, Albert Pujols, Xerxes, Sandra Day O'Connor, Eminem, Hillary Rodham Clinton, Ernest Gaines, Che Guevara, and Rachael Ray. He attended Antioch College, where he majored in English and communications. He currently lives in Houston, Texas, with his partner of 21 years, three cats, and a dog named Junie B.